MENTAL FRAMEWORKS
FOR OUR MODERN
REVOLUTION

MENTAL FRAMEWORKS FOR OUR MODERN REVOLUTION

CHANGE YOUR MIND IF YOU WANT TO CHANGE THE WORLD

ARIANE IVANIER

NEW DEGREE PRESS

MENTAL FRAMEWORKS FOR OUR MODERN REVOLUTION

Change Your Mind If You Want to Change the World

ISBN   978-1-63676-723-9 *Paperback*
        978-1-63730-044-2   *Kindle Ebook*
        978-1-63730-146-3   *Ebook*

To changemakers of the past, present, and future.

CONTENTS

INTRODUCTION

In the spring of 2020, I was one of the millions of students sent home from college. Suddenly, instead of getting to live in a dorm down the hall from my best friends, going to parties, being involved in incredible organizations, or taking classes with world-class professors, I was now paying tens of thousands of dollars to lie in my childhood bed and log onto Zoom.

Needless to say, the feeling of "life isn't what it's meant to be" was palpable. Then, when I thought the world couldn't change more, that I was living through one of the thickest chapters in tomorrow's history books—well, things changed again.

In just the first six months of 2020, we've faced plenty of historical moments.

A pandemic, cause by a virus, brings the entire world to a screeching halt.

A video of a man kneeling on the neck of another man forces people to say enough is enough.

An election year reminds us of our constitutional right to take a look at our country and decide whether or not we want to make a change.

The changes happening in the world seem so intense, especially contrasted to the feeling of life in our personal realities. If I looked out the window, I saw the world becoming a new place, bending and molding under the weight of historical event after historical event. Yet, I sat in my room, like so many others, as my days blurred together. Every day felt like a repeat of the last, and my entire self-evolution felt like it had come to a complete stop.

So, while I've seen people call this year the "year of the virus," the "year of the revolution," the "year where everything went to shit," I have found myself, as the pretentious student that I am, calling it "2020: the year of the paradox."

And I think this very paradox is what made everything so impactful. Everything was so contradictory and made people pay attention.

When progressives, advocates, activists, students, parents, and teachers took the streets and called for action, the country listened more than ever before. People talked about the Black Lives Matter movement on news networks across the country. Corporations released statements. Curious citizens watched documentaries and read books and engaged in conversations around the topic of real equity.

And the moment was led by progressives; by so many of generation Z—my generation, the ambassadors of change, the guiding light for a new day coming.

We have a broken democracy. The division, the cycles of poverty, the dysfunctional political systems, the misinformation, the lack of trust in institutions, the systems that seem to be built for some and broken for the rest—we have a broken democracy inside a broken country.

Almost half of eligible voters didn't vote in the 2016 election. Fifty-six percent of Black Americans do not have confidence in the police, and just by September of 2020, Black people have been 28 percent of the total killed by the police despite only being 13 percent of the population.[1] People distrust their media and their leaders, with only 41 percent of Americans having a "great deal" or "fair amount" of trust in the news.[2] And 64 percent of Americans have a hard time knowing when elected officials are being truthful when they speak.[3]

You start to think about one problem, and then another, and then another, and then another.... The stats I just laid out are just the tip of the iceberg, brief anecdotal examples of the ways in which our systems fail the collective people.

That's why I write this book: for anyone who considers themselves progressive, and for anyone who sees there are systemic issues in our country and wants to do something.

Ranging from the people who think they already do everything they can because they go to protests every weekend and study to work in a job that helps others, to the people

---

1   "Police Violence Map," Mapping Police Violence, accessed July 15, 2020.
2   Megan Brenan, "Americans' Trust in Mass Media Edges Down to 41%."
3   Lee Rainie, Scott Keeter, and Andrew Perrin, "Americans' Trust in Government, Each Other, Leaders."

who are overwhelmed and don't feel like they'll ever be able to do anything that truly makes a difference—this book is for you.

We are in a time of reckoning, a time where no one can accept that this is just "the way the country is." And despite so many disagreements and polarization and hatred, most are united in feeling there is something wrong going on right now. Along with that realization comes a feeling of utter hopelessness.

But when you watch these massive movements and you get to the core of it, you can find hope. That hope is in the people who participate in these quests for change: people who are spreading awareness via social media, people who are running for local and federal positions, people who are community organizers, people who start their own organizations in their local communities.

It's true as you learn more you discover the hopelessness and the horror of how systematic and entrenched our issues are. But you also find hope in the resilience of those who do not accept the failures of our system.

Because even if systems are broken and things are messed up beyond belief, there will always be someone who is calling for action against these injustices. I believe, and I know I'm not the only one, that we are on the precipice of something big: the creation of a new country. We just have to see that, ultimately, our real strength comes from the humanity of the moment and the core unifier of personhood in a movement.

There are so many people who don't know how to take part in this movement, and there are so many people who feel put off by the constant work that happens with no change coming through. I find hope in the collective movement of people who fight for change. But equally as important, I think there is power in the single human, and I know each individual can make an active revolutionary change by changing within.

I think there is something that we all *can* do and we all *must* do; it is easy to do, yet the most difficult to accomplish. We *can* change the way we think. We *must* change our minds.

I believe that in our fervid determination to change the world, we have forgotten about the work needed within ourselves. And I believe if we don't acknowledge this and actively work on it, we ultimately won't build the better world we claim to want. That's where this book's subject of mental frameworks comes in.

Your mental frameworks set up the way you perceive the world. It's the way your mind processes things. Everyone's mental frameworks are different due to different contexts and cultures and backgrounds, all things that affect and person-alize each person's mind and view of life. Too often we think of the way that we view the world as just simple facts, when in reality it is solely your personal truth, a truth that has been built and continues to be molded by your background and life experiences.

A mental framework is malleable, and that is powerful. The very notion of this fact gives truth to the idea that each indi-vidual has the power to change.

Sometimes, however, particularly in progressive spaces, we get too caught up in the change that the people around us need to undertake that we forget about the internal work that must be continually done within us to have mental frameworks that dismantle rather than uphold our institutions.

Our mental frameworks surrounding key issues need to be altered and changed. Otherwise, we are at risk of either never reaching real progress or reaching a version of progress riddled with different versions of our same problems.

The mental frameworks we must change are easy to understand, but they can be difficult to alter. But you can both understand them and begin modifying them by first recognizing three crucial areas that require a change in how we think about them. The way we view these crucial topics, the "Big Three," currently causes a lot of harm and perpetuates many systematic problems in our society. And these are the three main issues I will be addressing in the book. They are as follows:

1. Our frameworks of history—learning to view our history and historical figures as nuanced figures, not heroes or villains.
2. Our frameworks of our country's geographical makeup—learning how to grapple with the fact that we are a country made up of different cultures and people, none of which are more or less superior to one another.
3. Our framework of the binary—learning how to fight the urge to view things in black and white.

I write about these three issues because they are things that are not addressed nearly enough. They are issues I have seen almost everyone take part in, and I'm not saying that in any kind of accusatory way. I write this book as a love letter to people who are deeply invested in the work of advocacy and activism, and I bring forward the issue of adjusting the way our mental frameworks view the above three subjects because I believe it will ultimately do good in the work for revolutionary change.

You see, it doesn't just come from protests, hashtags, books, movies, and press releases that address these issues from big corporations. I'm not negating the power of those things. All of that is incredibly effective in raising attention. It tells the world that there is a problem we can't ignore and are refusing to silence.

But this kind of work also has its limits. It is a reactionary behavior, acting in response to when things go wrong. It's not creating something new or progressing to something different. And because it's so obvious and exposed to the public, it makes us, and subsequently, everyone around us, think that once the loud thing is done, the problem is solved. (Easy example: Barack Obama is elected president, whoop! Racism is over!)

But we know that isn't true. More has to be done. Quiet, internal work has to be done.

We are in the modern revolution, a time where people are fed up and no longer accepting our current reality as a fixed version of what is "normal." People want something new. People of different age groups, cultures, parties, races, genders—it doesn't matter—all feel collectively that "this isn't the ideal country I want." And I know that "we the people" are not just demanding change but are prepared to do something to make a change.

Our modern revolution will not be won through battles of bloodshed, or a collective uprising, or an overthrowing of a system. It's a revolution fought and won internally, then reflected externally. In other words, when we change our minds, when we change how we think, we will also change how we act. And when we change how we act, we impact the world around us. Our revolution of global change starts with humans changing from within.

A lot of people, when I first told them I was writing this book, asked me why I wanted to write it. Why did I think my voice added anything of value or substance to the conversation?

I wrote this book because I had a realization one day that sometimes I don't push myself to change since I'm so convinced I'm on the "right side" simply for being more lib-eral-minded. Because I understand the idea of systematic injustice, I don't stop and think about how I may contribute or uphold the very institutions I criticize.

This led me down a path of brainstorming where I came up with three limiting mental frameworks that I personally recognized I had and saw many others have in our country. I did research on those subjects to understand them and formulate a real theory of why it is so necessary for us to alter our frameworks when it comes to these topics. I explored the subjects of history, relationships, and binary thinking through the minds and lives of people who are experts on the subjects.

In this book, you'll learn, just as I did, how a professor came to realize what it meant to valuably teach history, how a psychologist applies theories of evolutionary psychology to the world we live in today, how different students form opinions of the regions in this country, and how a Rabbi realized his community had broken into "sides."

I wanted to explore the idea of personal responsibility and internal work to help externally change the world. I wrote this book so I could personally work through my own frameworks of our country and of the people within it. It was revolutionary, for me at least, to learn about the power of internal change; the potentiality of pushing my mind to explore nuance and critically think about the world around me; to remind myself that my perceptions of the world are not automatically correct, even if I do think of myself as a progressive or liberal or smart person.

I will be honest, though: At the age I am and the time we live in, it's scary to put my thoughts out there. It's weird to put words into the world under dramatic titles like "revolution" and "changing the world." But I put those big and flashy words in here because that's kind of my point. Even though the idea of changing your own mind might seem small, I think believing that will negate the power each individual holds.

In a time like this where every day seems like we are in a new chapter of history and where there are so much news and so many events and stories coming at us from all sides, it can be hard to realize that the biggest, boldest, and most world-changing thing to do is recognize ourselves as part of the complex and massive tapestry that is our world and our time right now.

Each person has an effect, and I argue that revolutionary change comes from individuals acknowledging that and working to ensure that an internal framework matches the external vision of a better world.

Maybe my words will fall to deaf ears or no ears at all, but if what I'm writing makes just one person readjust their thinking, like researching and writing this book helped me do, then I think it will have been worth it. Because I know that if I helped change one person, then I took part in the revolution and I helped change the world.

Ultimately, this comes down to the fact that I believe in the power of the human condition and the human mind, not as an infallible thing, but rather a malleable one that is able to adapt and evolve to help us become better.

We each have the power to change the world. We first just have to change our minds.

PART I

CHANGING YOUR MIND

CHAPTER 1

HOW YOU CAN CHANGE

———

The very idea of the book, the titular concept, might seem dramatic to some. I mean, any time you use phrases like "changing the world" it has an immediate grandiose energy, and I will admit I love flare for drama's sake. But I also really believe there is massive potential in the ability and choice to change your mind; to understand that you as an individual hold power in society and how your mind, something that wholly belongs to you and is controlled by you, can have an impact on the change that occurs all around you.

PEOPLE ARE THE ANSWER

When I was first trying to get a more focused idea for this book, I interviewed a lot of people. Some researchers, academics, activists...all people I wanted to speak with to get a more focused idea of what, specifically, I wanted to write about when it comes to advocacy in today's environment. I spoke to people who all had some sort of expertise on subjects of advocacy and progress and things I knew I was interested in talking about. But the focused idea of mental frameworks didn't really come about until I interviewed a couple from Chicago.

They made me realize what it means to be a person who has truly lived. Many people think 2020 is special because of its clear role in history. But we forget that every single person and moment is creating history.

I spoke to these two incredibly accomplished individuals. Marv Hoffman is a lifelong educator, the founding director of the University of Chicago's first charter school and one of the founders of the University's Urban Teacher Education Program—all that on top of the books and widely published articles that he's written.

Rosellen Brown is an author renowned for her works of stories and poems. One of her books, *Before and After*, was adapted into a major motion picture. Rosellen is also an educator, teaching English and creative writing.

I was prepared to speak to them about many things related to education and advocacy and had lots of questions ready for a traditional thirty-minute professional interview.

In the end, I spoke to this couple for over an hour. After the first ten minutes, I had completely abandoned all my questions, preferring to just engage these thoughtful people in conversation.

They told me their life stories: what it was like going to school while the Civil Rights movement was in full swing; how they had experienced life and people from all corners of this country, like Mississippi, New York, Houston, and Chicago; and how each of their paths and goals in life were crashing into the realities of the context of the country.

Marv studied psychology and then ended up ir.
because President Johnson started the anti-pov
ment. One of the cornerstones was the Head Star\
which Marv worked for. Rosellen's success came fr(
and stories, many of which were inspired by the   ....y
around her. These two did all this while raising kids. They've
experienced life and people and history.

When I interviewed them, I was still at the research and
brainstorming part of my book. I knew there was something
I wanted to say, but it felt more like I had thousands of ideas
just bumping around in my mind and not really sure how
to articulate exactly what I was thinking.

Marv and Rosellen did not come to the conversation to just
answer questions about themselves, thank goodness. Because
they asked me questions and engaged me in conversation
that helped me better understand the real focus of my work.

"What drives you?" they asked me.

"Why do you think your perspective is unique on this subject?"

I gathered up my jumbled thoughts to answer the impressive
people on my computer screen. I explained to them how vis-
ceral it feels to be a young adult living in this time. I told them
my desire to figure out how we can make the world a truly
better place; my fears of reactionary politics and progressives;
how I worried that, unless advocacy changed its tune or at
least acknowledged the missing parts of the field, we could
end up with a world that isn't a better place but rather just a
distorted version of what we have today.

I told them about how, so often, it felt like people's approach to advocacy wasn't including internal mental work that each individual has to do. How, because we live in a society where prejudice and bias and the urge to oversimplify everything is within the system, everyone, no matter their status of most to least "woke," has to do internal work to undo those systems. I told them how I didn't see how the conversation around creating long-lasting real change hasn't included the work people have to do to change themselves and the way they view certain things.

Marv and Rosellen chuckled at what I was saying. "It's kind of crazy. When we were your age, we never would have been as concerned or cared enough to be knowledgeable about half the things you're talking about. But the younger generations are so involved now."

"I guess so," I responded. "I just feel so acutely aware of the history I'm living in, and the pivotal moments just seem to keep happening. And I keep thinking about how useless and powerless I so often feel in these movements and in history! But it's not true, is it? Each of us has individual power and an impact."

This couple, who had signed up for a formal interview about their lives, was all of a sudden part of my brainstorming process.

"There's no doubt. Everything is interconnected. Moments in history meet up with your private intimate self and life, and each impact one another," they said.

I nodded and took vigorous notes on a sticky note app on my laptop.

"So, I'm being influenced by the world just by existing, and no matter what I do, my existence will influence the world in return."

"Right."

Talking with them, I didn't realize it yet, was my first time articulating my theory on the importance of our mental frameworks in advocacy. I didn't say it with as much precision, and I didn't come away from the meeting with my thesis statement, but there was something about speaking and seeing Marv and Rosellen that unlocked the entire idea behind what I wanted to say.

I was talking to this couple, looking at these two people on who had experienced so much life and who had the marks of history in their life stories. They lived lives and created narratives that were woven with the Civil Rights movement, the Watergate scandal, the end of the Cold War, 9/11, the technological revolution, COVID-19, this current Black Lives Matter movement…and it put everything into perspective.

I had been so busy thinking about this current moment of loud calls for progress. All the time during 2020, I feel like I talked about the fact that we were living in history and how insane that all is. But the reality is that we are always living in history.

Looking back on it now, I think this interview is where I just got to know these two people, and they got to know me. It made me have such a breakthrough because it helped remind me of the importance of the individual. Talking to them made me realize that world events and governments and media change all around us. And ultimately, we can't really have much say in what happens. But what we do have a say in, all the time, for the whole time we walk this earth, is ourselves. We are always creating history and being part of the fabric of time.

It doesn't matter if you become nationally known or you're just a person who interacts with friends and family. Everything you do affects everything around you. No matter what, your footprint will be in history and your impact will be felt in the future. And as such everything we do and every action we take or decision we make or mindset we have impacts ourselves, impacts our current world, and impacts our future.

The way we create fundamental change is by changing ourselves. And we change ourselves by changing our perspectives of one another and the country around us.

HOW CAN MINDS CHANGE?

Once I started to understand what I was trying to articulate, I wanted to do a bit more research on the idea of "changing ourselves as an individual." I wanted to understand how one can do this and whether it's really as powerful as I was starting to think it was.

One book that helped explain and simplify the science behind how a mind can change is *Algorithms to Live By: The Computer Science of Human Decisions* by Brian Christian and Tom Griffiths. This book talks about how algorithms of computer science can be utilized in figuring out how the human mind functions. Don't worry, I won't get too technical and go into STEM jargon, but I do want to briefly speak about the general concept of the book, as I found it connected strongly to my idea of frameworks.

This book is an example of how when we zoom out and examine the human mind, we begin to see how it can apply to so many different disciplines. We can explain it through psychology, neuroscience, philosophy, computer science, and spirituality, as just a few examples. It's a thing that can be analyzed, deconstructed, and theorized. We don't spend enough time taking advantage of that.

In the introduction to the book, Christian and Griffiths write, "Thinking algorithmically about the world, learning about fundamental structures of the problems we face and about the properties of their solutions, can help us see how good we actually are, and better understand the errors that we make."[4]

Although "thinking algorithmically about the world" may sound complex and should only be done by people who frequently think about the word algorithm, as a person who makes an active effort to stay away from words of that nature,

---

4   Brian Christian and Tom Griffiths, *Algorithms to Live By: The Computer Science of Human Decisions*, 4–5.

I'm telling you it has value and is not as difficult to understand as it may sound.

It's simply talking about applying ideas of computer science to our thought process. And isn't "learning about fundamental structures of the problems we face and about the properties of their solution" kind of the whole idea? There are systemic issues. It's not just a few bugs that have to be addressed—there's a whole virus in the unit.

I use this example just to show another form of how our minds are malleable and how we can use them to create real change—starting with ourselves, which will then reflect into the world as you and the world around you are in constant interaction, creating one another.

So, you can think about the concepts in whatever way make the most sense for you. Personally, I feel most comfortable when I think of it plainly explained like: "Here's how we think about this certain thing, and why that thought process is causing issues. If we thought about this thing in this different way instead, there are so many ways that this small difference can make a real impact in not only how we think but how we act."

POSITIONALITY

Something we need to acknowledge before talking more specifically about mental frameworks is this concept of positionality. Positionality is a theory that is a part of epistemology, the philosophy that studies how individuals know what they know.

Positionality is the context that you live in every day because of who you are in society. It is "the social and political context that creates your identity in terms of race, class, gender, sexuality, and ability status. Positionality also describes how your identity influences, and potentially biases, your understanding of and outlook on the world."[5]

Your family, your race, your culture, the neighborhood you grew up in, the schooling you received, the friendships you make, and even the person you bumped into on the street ten minutes ago are all things that affect your formation and your position in the world. And all of them affect your mental frameworks.

MENTAL FRAMEWORKS

When we were kids and my mom wanted to go to visit museums on vacation, my sister would quietly agree and be a pleasant kid for my parents. She would engage in conversation about the contents of the museum and would keep her grievances of boredom to a minimum. Me, on the other hand? I had decided it was my duty to make sure I made clear how terrible a time I was having, and that the contents of the museum were unequivocally the most boring things to have ever been on God's green Earth.

My sister is the person I am most genetically similar to. She and I grew up in almost the exact same circumstances, and we have experienced many of the same things in life. Despite these facts, we saw a trip to a museum completely differently

---

5   Dictionary.com, s.v. "Positionality."

because there is so much around us that affects our brains and our personalities and our positionalities. Therefore, as similar as my sister and I are, we still have different minds and mental frameworks and experience starkly different worlds. In turn, that makes us have different thoughts and actions for things.

Despite the common saying of "you are not the center of the universe," in some ways, you kind of are. Every person is different because of their positionality. They see the world and experience the world in completely different ways, which means each person is living in their own version of a world with their own unique mental frameworks.

Mental frameworks are "an explanation and representation of a person's thought process (cognition) for how something works in the real world (external reality)."[6] Basically, it's how we process the world. It's what forms our thoughts, which leads to the formation of opinions and formations of actions.

Dan Cloer wrote an article, "Rethinking Our Mental Frameworks," explaining concepts of mental frameworks and how minds are malleable.

> *LeDoux offers his best estimate: "Life requires many brain functions, functions require systems, and systems are made of synoptically connected neurons. We all have the same brain systems, and the number of neurons in each brain system is more or less the same in each of us as well. However, the particular*

---

6   David Sammon, "Understanding Sense-Making," *Encyclopedia of Decision Making and Decision Support Technologies*, ed. by Adam Frédéric and Patrick Humphreys, 916–921.

way those neurons are connected is distinct, and that
uniqueness, in short, is what makes us who we are."[7]

You have neurons firing in your brain that cause you to think the way you do and cause someone else to think the way they do. It's not some intrinsic natural force pulling one person to good or bad or dumb or smart. Mental frameworks have been changed and altered because of each unique life a person lives.

It's difficult because the human brain is such an insane creation. "Everything happens so naturally," Cloer writes. "Through heredity and experience, every human brain becomes uniquely 'wired.' This wiring allows our minds to physically function; we perceive, integrate, store and retrieve, all without realizing we are doing it."[8]

It's not like any of us are cognizant of the ways in which we are processing the world around us. We don't think about processing; we just process.

The conclusion of Cloer's article, as well as his take on LeDoux's work is that "you are what you think."[6] This is a powerful statement, and it can be very freeing. We can remember that we are these things that are shaped and formed uniquely and able to change.

We know our minds are malleable, and as such, we as a whole are malleable. We are able to change because we are able to change the way we think.

---

7   Dan Cloer, "Rethinking Our Mental Framework."
8   Ibid.

"It is heartening to understand that the human mind has the capacity to change. We are not fated to a hard-wired future or inescapably doomed to a downhill run. We experience, learn and act. We have the capacity to evaluate the consequences of our behavior."[6]

I use the concept of mental frameworks to help remind myself that the way I view the world—the way that I experience things, the thoughts I have, the things I say—is not some set-in-stone fact that everyone else is experiencing. Sure, it's my reality and my truth, but my view is not a objective perception of the world. No one experiences this version of the world, and everyone else's version is different. And that can be scary, but it's also incredibly heartening when you realize that, as Cloer wrote, "the human mind has the capacity to change."

I have taken this idea that we are able to change as my inspiration. We all know there's a problem, and we know we want to do something about it. And if you're able to change personally to contribute to a better holistic future, why wouldn't you?

A SIMULTANEOUS FORM OF ADVOCACY

The problem is there is so much dangerous, violent, and loud terrible shit going on in our world. It's hard to think we can solve the issue by "changing our minds" when we clearly need to make loud noise to get the public's attention. We have a broken democracy: corrupt politicians, people being killed, unbreakable cycles of poverty…so many things that, in the moment, cannot be saved by changing our minds.

However, I firmly believe that we have to have a simultaneous form of advocacy. Advocating with protests or backlash or social media campaigns is completely necessary. We should never be silent and show complacency to corruption, violence, or discrimination. But this form of advocacy is typically only reactionary—acting in reaction to all the aforementioned bad shit. Changing our mental frameworks allows us to build something new simultaneously. It's working to create a better world while also fighting against the immediate crisis that occurs.

Advocacy that is done through constant effort to change our mental frameworks is the work that must be done to ensure the "better tomorrow" we fight for is something different and truly better. When we work to change our mental frameworks and readjust how we see our country, its citizens, and our society, then this is a type of advocacy that allows us to take responsibility for ourselves as part of the greater tapestry of overall progress.

It's advocacy that comes from bettering ourselves, understanding that change comes from growth, and knowing that change is always possible.

Changing our mental frameworks is hard, and it can be tempting to skip over the real need for each of us to do this work. It can be so easy to assure ourselves that our framework on the world is correct and doesn't need to be altered. But we all exist in a world set up to perpetuate inequity. Frankly, if you were raised in this country, despite your best intentions and ability to educate yourself, it's almost impossible there isn't still internal work you need to do.

Despite how easy it is to write off the need to do this work and undermine the importance of it, I implore you, I implore myself, I implore all of us to not skip over it. If we don't change our core thought processes on the important things, like the subjects I delve into in this book, I am not sure we will ever create something new. We will simply always react to the atrocities of the world, not work to build something better by building a better people.

By changing the way we think, we change the way we act, we change the way we treat one another, and we change the way we view our country. The internal change reflects in external progress.

It's why the title of my book says that this book is for the "modern revolution" because what I believe is the tool to creating a different and better future is changing the way we think about fundamental things.

Our modern revolution is one that comes from giving power to thought, to the mind, and ultimately to the belief that each individual choosing to reframe their mind makes way for us to reframe our world.

When we change our minds, we change ourselves, and we change others. When we change others, we change humanity.

And that starts with you.

CHAPTER 2

THE POWER OF
A PERSON

———

The year 2020 has been one of horrors and sadness. It has led to sickness and loneliness and death. It has forced us out of our preconceived notions of normalcy. College students went from sleeping in dorms to sleeping ten steps away from their parents' bedroom. The news went from something that droned on in the background to something that would announce death counts. Grocery store outings went from nuisance trips to the only opportunity to leave the house. One day life was one way, the next it wasn't.

WHAT IS NORMAL, AND WHY IN THE WORLD WOULD WE WANT TO GO BACK?

Something that was commonly said throughout all this, from the ads on TV to the conversations I would have with friends to the endless social media posts:

"I can't wait for us to go back to normal."

Then over the summer, there was a massive civil rights movement after the deaths of George Floyd and Breonna Taylor, a racial reckoning that made millions of people reassess the systematic issues of our country that lead to institutionalized racism.

For me, this moment was combined with my other personal experiences. I was getting more involved in many internships and advocacy groups that were focused on the necessary change this country needs to undergo. I started to get more invested both on a professional and personal level with communities that are constantly fighting for massive change in this country.

In response to the idea of "going back to normal," I think I, and many, many others, started reassessing the true merits of the "normal" people were so desperate to get back to.

The increasing understanding of our country's issues helped shape my perspective and inspire me to write this book. The year 2020 was not a shit year that we should forget and move on from. Instead, it should be the year where we all finally woke up, and as a nation, as a people, decided that we were no longer going to tolerate what we previously accepted as conventional.

What was ordinary before 2020? What led to the volatile country that we exist in today? What led to the three mental frameworks that I break down in this book—relationship with our past, the way we view one another and group one another, and binary thinking—to become so toxic?

In 2018, Jeremy W. Peters wrote "In a Divided Era, One Thing Seems to Unite: Political Anger" for the *New York Times,* and he explains how and why tensions are higher now than ever before. He offers many anecdotal examples of couples breaking up because of political views, familial relationships being torn apart, and people yelling at one another, crying, and even sometimes resorting to violence.

"High tension, raw emotion, and occasional violence have always been a feature of American democracy—in times of war and peace, through presidential impeachments and mass protest movements," Peters writes. "But interviews with voters across the country, along with an analysis of recent research by political scientists who specialize in the partisan division, suggest that politics is changing how Americans think and behave in new and unsettling ways."[9]

Peters points out that this theme of high tension and fear and competition has always been a staple of our politics, but today it's something different, something more extreme. We're not seeing something that is just "of this generation" that will naturally fade out. We're seeing partisanship and division that is leading the country in a dangerous direction.

And we have to find a way to go beyond just recognizing that anger, to actually reconciling with what those feelings are and where and how they can be best distributed.

Systematic problems have always been there. Systems are built into the foundation of this country to disenfranchise most and bolster a very few. But there is no denying that we

---

9   Jeremy W. Peters, "In a Divided Era, One Thing Seems to Unite: Political Anger."

are living at a crucial boiling point for our country. Where the way these systems have failed has become more obvious and the consequences more dire.

In a time where our access to information and opportunity is almost at an overload, we've allowed ourselves to simplify things around us in an effort to easily process everything. The ability to appreciate nuance and fight plain narratives has become increasingly difficult, and it has led us to easily accept mental frameworks that oversimplify everything around us.

I no longer want to contribute to that kind of country. I no longer want to have the mental frameworks that operate within these systems and uphold this toxic mindset. Because I've seen, or am just beginning to see, how that leads to the worst in us and leads to a country that stands for hate, division, and violence rather than the ideals we are meant to strive for: life, liberty, and the pursuit of happiness.

IT'S NEVER SIMPLE

If there's one thing I want people to take away from this book, firstly, it's to start understanding and valuing the power that comes from the individual.

As humans, we have the capacity to change.

As humans, we affect the world around us just by being humans who are a part of the world.

And the world is filled with billions of complex people who have the capacity to change.

We can't forget the power that exists in these facts. We all have innate power because of the individual impact we all have and the choice we can always make to modify ourselves and constantly work to be the best version of ourselves possible.

Secondly, understanding and valuing this innate power that comes from the complicated individual human will help us stop viewing one another and the world around us as just these simple narratives.

The three mental frameworks I talk about in this book are our relationship with our past, the way we view one another and group one another, and binary thinking. You'll start to realize, as you read more in detail about these frameworks, there is a common theme.

The common theme is that we like to simplify everything into digestible narratives. We like to boil something down to something that is easy to understand, stripping it of all its nuance. It's an incredibly limiting way of thinking and, as you'll see, it does nothing to actually advance us toward progress.

A GLOBAL PANDEMIC REVEALS SHIT ABOUT HUMANITY

I have existed in a place of great privilege during the pandemic. I haven't lost any close friends or family, and my family was not terribly affected by the economic hit. But, of course, the events happening around still rocked me.

The tipping point we've been inching slowly toward as we become more polarized and fractured perfectly coincided with a global pandemic. There was no turning back. We won't be going back to normal, so we have to fight now to create a better normal.

This year has shown the power people have to overcome, to resist, to fight back, to endure. We've all seen something truly unprecedented with the pandemic, the Black Lives Matter movement, and the work from activists and advocacy groups to campaign in an election like never before. None of that came about naturally. It came about from sheer force of will.

But this year has also revealed people's true weaknesses: how people desire power and fear what happens when traditional power structures are questioned or toppled. We've seen people brandishing guns and calling for law and order when they really mean segregation and violence. I've watched videos on how young kids fall down an alt-right pipeline because they come across unfiltered content from extremists who play on their insecurities, luring them into terrorism.

And all of this has led me to realize that we can think about one another in two ways:

1. Some people are just naturally good (i.e., they fight for human rights, wear masks, and speak against corrupt politicians) and others are naturally bad (i.e., they say ignorant things and refuse to give up their guns).

2. No human is inherently good or bad.

I choose to believe the second option, which is so much harder to do as the easy answer is to label "good" or "evil."

It's a soothing idea that we simply have to "defeat the bad people" to get "back to the good times." But that isn't how it works and it ignores the realities of systematic issues that we all contribute to, in one way or another, consciously or not.

The real way forward is to question and investigate the toxic mindsets that lead to inequity, hatred, disparity, and ultimately, a dysfunctional society.

Now to people who think they already do this or that their framework of the world is already in tip-top shape, good for you! Truly. But my fear is there are too many people (especially those claiming the title of progressives) who are so adamant they are on "the right side of history" and they stand and fight for what is right that they don't stop to consider how all of their actions unconsciously, as well as consciously, contribute to issues.

I've spoken to many, many, many people who are leftists or progressives or liberals or democrats, whatever title you want to throw on it, and explained to them my mental framework theory. And often, they end up telling me they never considered how these mindsets might be corrosive and certainly never thought about how they contribute to the upholding of systems they speak so eagerly about dismantling.

Hell, I myself never considered the things I wrote about in this book and how my own frameworks were contributing to the problem until I took a minute to reflect on myself. Before, I was very comfortable going about the world thinking I was helping the "good" side because of who I surround myself with and who I vote for in elections. But, unfortunately, it is just not that simple.

POLITICS AND FANTASY NOVELS

A fun fact about me is that I love fantasy books. This past year I took a year off school and moved to DC. When you decide to do this in the middle of a pandemic, there really isn't much you can do. When I'm not doing work for my internships, I have a lot of time on my hands. And I fill those hours by reading—a lot. To mark my accomplishment when I finished a book, I put the book on the windowsill in my apartment, growing my collection of "books I read while the world was ending, and I moved to DC to work in politics and advocacy because I've decided that I want to have gray hair at the age of thirty-five." The collection started August 20, and as I sit here on January 29, the number stands at twenty-two.

If you were to look at my book collection as an outsider who doesn't know anything about me, you would have a hard time pinning down what the common theme is. Because the two types of books lined up along the wall are young adult fantasy and political books, which typically isn't the most common combination. But personally, I found a common theme between those two—a theme that sort of led me to where I am today, writing this book about the need for frameworks that push away our constant desire for simple narratives.

When I was younger, I would make up stories and live in imaginary worlds; stories of worlds in the sky, of eternal kings who lived in dark corners, and queens who were Gods. I used to resent the idea of the "regular" world, hating the mundane nature of our repetitive lives, and wished I could enter one of my secret worlds instead.

A huge reason for this was because I was drawn to the idea of living in a world with a cohesive and adventurous narrative. I wanted the heroes to be obvious and the villains scary but ultimately destined to fail. And the reason I got involved in politics at first was because if there's one field of work that pretends to exist in this narrative, it's politics. Politics is all horserace and excitement over victories and losses. One party is a hero and the other is a villain.

So, when Donald Trump was elected President, he was the catalyst for my passion in politics because he is the living embodiment of turning politics into a digestible story. Trump is like a cartoon: A person who does nothing to try to evoke humanity and is comfortable as a caricature. So, when Trump was elected, suddenly, I was in the first chapter of my hero's quest and my story had a clear villain.

I specifically remember going to the gym on November 9, 2016 and looking around and thinking about how insane it was that there was probably a big group of people here who had just voted for Donald Trump. I was scared. I couldn't stop thinking about how there were people in that gym who were just running on the treadmill or lifting weights who were racist; who didn't like seeing two people of the same gender hold hands; who wanted to control my reproductive system.

This really, really pissed me off. Obviously because I believe in the opposite ideology, but honestly, I was mostly pissed that people could get away with having these thoughts, with fitting the narrative that I had assigned to them as the "villain," but they were able to live among me. There was no sign above them that said, "I voted for Trump because I liked how he talked about that girl in that tape," nor were they actively walking up to me, trying to draw me into a fight where my sixteen-year-old intellectual superiority could best them in an argument.

On that day in November, I wanted to join politics to unmask and defeat the evil. I was the protagonist, and the United States was my new world, a country on the brink of dystopia, waiting for the brave and noble heroes to come to defend her.

But here's the thing: Although the storybook element of politics is what drew me in, it's not why I've stayed. Once I actually chose to get involved in organizations and community spaces, I started to see this incredible underbelly. The people in realms of advocacy and liberal politics, who chose a life of public service to genuinely try to make a difference; people who decide that no matter how hard it is or how little things make sense and how difficult it is to change minds or change things in the country; they still wake up every single day and choose to try. There is something so wonderfully and beautifully noble about that utterly human choice so many in public service make.

And when I took a few moments to truly reflect on why I love the fantasy books I spend so many hours reading, I found that the same thing is true. It's the display of humanity that keeps me enthralled in these books, not the fantasy worlds. It's Harry asking Lupin about his parents in *Harry Potter and the Prisoner of Azkaban*; it's Kaz refusing to cure his leg to remind him of the promise he made his brother in *Six of Crows*; it's Ead giving up her chance for ultimate glory to return to save Sabran in *The Priory of the Orange Tree*.[10][11][12] It's the idea that no matter the world or the powers or the characters, there is this common humanity that I can relate to.

So maybe it's the imaginary worlds in my fantasy books that catch my attention and lead me to open the book and turn the page, just like maybe it's a cartoon villain who becomes president that places me in the trenches of the political world. But it's not what makes me stay. What makes me turn to the next page and choose to fight another day is the humanity on display.

I didn't realize any of this until I was actually reflecting on what led me to write this book. And then I saw that, despite the simple narratives, the digestible hero's arc, and the enticing made-up worlds might be what draws people in, the personhood is what holds the real power.

That, combined with all the events of the past year, drove me to write this book on this subject. Because I know despite everything that may tell us otherwise, ultimately our strongest power comes from within ourselves, the choices we make, the people we decide to be, and the way we choose

---

10   J.K. Rowling, *Harry Potter and the Prisoner of Azkaban.*

11   Leigh Bardugo, *Six of Crows.*

12   Samantha Shannon, *The Priory of the Orange Tree.*

to view the world. We have so much potential of making a difference through our own selves.

We all know the issues of this world cannot be fixed through a piece of legislation or a different administration. Our disparities come from a system that is built to not serve the betterment of all. So, if the issue is systematic, you have to get to the root of it. And in that, you have to acknowledge you and your current state of mind are a part of the root problem. And if you take up the work to change yourself, you might see, slowly but surely, that change reflected in the world around you.

PART II

MENTAL FRAMEWORKS

CHAPTER 3

THERE IS NO TODAY WITHOUT YESTERDAY

———

The conversation around how we should view our history has recently become more prevalent. We've had protests and conversations on the monuments and statues around this country; protests against the very concept of Columbus Day; and questions around what the Fourth of July means, and who was truly free on this day of independence. All things that have led to a much-needed conversation around who the figures of our history are, how we treat our past, and whom and how we choose to honor.

In wake of this, however, I've noticed a lot of people swinging completely toward the defense of our nation's past or swinging completely the other direction by viewing our history with only shame and trying to erase moments and people of the past.

A TWITTER TALE: MILLENNIALS VS. GEN Z

I started thinking about the fact that in our current frameworks we have this obsession with vilifying things and how often we view the past as a holistic "bad" thing when I was doing one of my normal daily (hourly) activities: scrolling through Twitter.

I clicked on the Black Lives Matter trend and was scrolling. Footage of protests, tweets from celebrities, tweets about the tweets from celebrities, informative threads...the normal stuff. And then I saw a tweet that went along the lines of "Look at what Gen Z was able to do! Millennials weren't even able to make protests last a week for the deaths of Michael Brown and Eric Garner."

Beyond the fact this person seemed to be making a competition out of tragedy, it was just petty and ineffective. I stared at that tweet for a few minutes. I'm very used to people on Twitter being contradictory for the sake of contradiction, and normally I can just scroll past it. But for some reason, this time it really stuck with me.

It made me think about the wave of activism that had happened those few years back. The issue of police violence garnered massive national and media attention after the death of Trayvon Martin, Michael Brown, and Eric Garner by police officers or "wannabe" guys playing the role of vigilante. I was in middle school at the time. And coming from a fairly affluent white family and school, it was my first real exposure to police violence. I saw how social systems work for some but hurt others.

I remember the conversations that were happening around my school and around my dinner table. I knew of inequality and racism in our country, but I knew about it as a concept, not something that I interacted with, contributed to, or ever bore witness to. At the time, I think I assumed that if something "racist" was happening it would be someone overtly being hateful to someone because of the color of their skin. I hadn't had to grapple with the effects of racism in our systems of society. Before this moment I hadn't actively seen how institutions can have such a double standard and how that double standard is not only unjust but can be a direct threat to communities. As I grew older and became more educated and aware, I saw how that reality applies to housing and schooling and government districting and basically everything in our society, but this moment in 2014 was the catalyst for my understanding.

I know that my first exposure to the words "Black Lives Matter" was via social media in 2014. As such, my education and understanding of why these hashtags and these movements and these marches existed were spurred on because of that. I now have a greater understanding now than I did then. Not only because of age and natural maturity, but because of the big movement of activism in 2014 that brought attention to this issue.

What happened in 2014 is the reason why 2020 looks the way it did. Since 2014, social media has continued to spread and boom, making not only these deaths something that we see on a daily basis now, but also making our ability to reach out and organize easier. But the movement of 2020 would not exist without 2014, just like the movement of 2014 would not exist without all the other past moments of history and the millions of people who took part in it calling for justice and equity.

We must acknowledge context. The national awareness that was brought about from those initial protests as well as the establishment of the organization "Black Lives Matter" are the foundations on which the 2020 protests grew.

And that's just one example. Everything around us relates to what came before us. There is simply no way that we would be where we are today without the work that was done before-hand. We learn from the past; we take examples from history and apply them to where we are today.

Every moment stands on the shoulders of its historical pro-ceedings, for all the good and bad that might entail. If people in the past had not been there and then, fighting to make space for movements, there would be no movement today.

Now, of course, I'm looking at "history" in this example as something that happened six years ago, which I recognize is a very small-time difference, all things considered. It's a lot easier to give the people of 2014 respect and understanding as they are far more similar to us than people in the 1800s, for example.

But this moment just shed a light on two things that I want to discuss: 1) how we love to ignore context because the past con-text does not fit comfortably in our present narratives; and 2) how we have an obsession with pretending like things exist in a vacuum and our generations are isolated occurrences.

FOUNDING FATHERS: ICONS DESERVING OF A MUSICAL OR SLAVE-OWNING MONSTERS?

As another example, we can look at the conversation that circulates around *Hamilton,* the musical, and the subject of how to teach people about the way this nation was built. There are people who argue that because the fact that many of these men were, in reality, less like valiant heroes of war and more like power-hungry slave-owners, we shouldn't make or praise musicals that don't shed light on this reality. Others argue that our history is something miraculous and important, and we should showcase these men as some form of deity, and their shortcomings shouldn't be considered as it has nothing to do with the events of our history.

Here's the thing though—I really don't think that either of those options is correct and fully considers how the past is related to today.

The mental frameworks of our past are heavily entrenched with the frameworks we have with ourselves and our current generation. We need to change the way we look at things that happened beforehand, stop framing our history as narrative stories so they make more sense, and apply nuance and context to our history, as well as consider how we are formed from that history.

Our frameworks are formed because of the way we experience the world. Depending on the family you come from, the life experiences you have, the wealth you are born into or acquire, your gender, your race, your sexuality...all these things affect your mental frameworks of the world around you. Hell, the experience you had when you tripped and fell on the way to a coffee shop ultimately affects your framework. It's like the idea of the butterfly effect; it applies to who you are and your mental frameworks as well. Everything you do and say and experience forms you and forms your mind.

If we don't apply nuance to our history and we create stories where our history is made up of archetypal villains and heroes, then we run the risk of not accepting it as a part of our genuine human stories, and we don't properly learn from it.

PSYCHOLOGICALLY SPEAKING, IT'S NORMAL THAT YOU HATE POLITICS

Here is the biggest issue: Our brains don't like complicated things. That is simply the truth. I do not care how smart you are, psychologically speaking, we cannot handle processing a thousand complex things, and we prefer to process the simple narratives.

Alain Berthoz wrote about this idea for the series *Research and Perspectives in Neuroscience*s:

> *The human brain imposes, in a top-down fash-ion, its rules of interpretation on sensory data. It transforms the perceived world according to rules of symmetry, stability, and kinematic laws derived from principles of maximum smoothness. These rules follow simplifying principles that allow the simplification of neurocomputation to speed up*

action. Top-down controlled attention is also a powerful selector.[13]

Our psychological process means we simplify the world so we can interpret it. Even if we intellectually understand this is how our brain works, we begin to take the simplified versions of things in our brain as the reality of what that thing is in the external world. And this can lead to problems because things tend to be far more nuanced than the simplified versions in our mind.

David Green wrote an article, "Simple Thinking in a Complex World Is a Recipe for Disaster," to explore this very concept. Green writes,

> *For all our sophistication, we react to the world in simple ways. Our world is complex, but our ability to cope with it is limited. We seek simple solutions that hide or ignore the complexity [...] Our brains cope with complexity by identifying important features and filtering out unnecessary detail. On seeing that the space you enter has four walls, a floor, and a ceiling, you know you have entered a room and can usually ignore the details.*[14]

Green delves into why this simplification leads to shortcomings, explaining how as we receive more and more

---

13 Alain Berthoz, "The Human Brain 'Projects' upon the World, Simplifying Principles and Rules for Perception," in *Neurobiology of "Umwelt": How Living Beings Perceive the World*, ed. Alain Berthoz and Yves Christen, 17–27.

14 David Green, "Simple Thinking in a Complex World Is a Recipe for Disaster."

information in a world that is filled with constant and increasing access to information, more and more people are going to be seeking the simple answer to the confusing world around us.

And that, right there, is what we have to fight against when it comes to important things—like how we view our past. When we are learning about our history, our mental frameworks clump it all as a thing of the past that we aren't intrinsically linked to. We don't associate the past with who we are today. And we have to actively work to change our frameworks from doing this when it comes to certain things.

Dr. Glenn Geher is a psychologist, a professor, and an expert on evolutionary psychology. I was able to speak to him about these big concepts, and how they relate to psychology.

When I talked to him about advocacy and politics and my theory of mental frameworks, he explained to me how it fit into evolutionary psychology.

"Our minds did not evolve for large scale politics," Dr. Geher said. "Evolutionary study shows us that in the past politics were small scale."

He even talked about how this theory applied to the surprising Trump 2016 victory. "Trump's rhetoric and what he appealed to actually tapped into something primal within many of us. Tribalism, male dominance, protection, etc. His simplistic slogans and way of speech tapped into our desire for simple politics."

There's definitely a lot we can learn from that.

We have to, as Dr. Geher said, be aware of where certain behavior comes from. When things go wrong or people seem to be just downright evil, we shouldn't move to hatred of that person or that group or that movement. Rather, we should seek to explore where it comes from. What systems have been built that allow a toxic and destructive type of thinking or action to prevail?

BUT HOW DOES THIS RELATE TO OUR RELATIONSHIP WITH HISTORY?

I took a class last semester called "Gender from a Global Perspective." The typical class that makes an eighteen-year-old college freshman come back home and, in the words of my father, "all of a sudden have such annoying opinions." But all that aside, I remember learning about second-wave feminism and how white-washed the movement was; how it excluded women of color and propped up women who were basically as privileged as you could get while still having a uterus.

It was important for me to understand that so I can be aware that modern feminism as a movement and a title is founded in racism and ultimately took actions to enforce patriarchy rather than fully dismantling it. It was also important for me to see how women who came before me lived in a world that was so much harder to exist in as an independent person detached from societal expectations and the need for men. The things I fight for now are because of them. They did a lot of work, but I have to be part of the solution in places where they fell short.

In 1963 the US women's movements won things like the Equal Pay Act. The fight for the federal legalization of abortion was fought for tirelessly by women and resulted in the infamous 1973 Roe vs. Wade supreme court case.[15] Marital rape only became illegal in all fifty states in 1993.[16]

The flawed movements of the past still accomplished extraordinary things, and the fights I'm able to fight for today are because I stand on the shoulders of these movements. And there were absolute faults to those movements and to many, many of those leaders. The first event for women's rights is widely considered when suffragists gathered in Seneca Falls, New York, in July 1848, and they called for the right to vote. But to be clear, they were calling for the right of white women to vote. No black women were invited. This is a common theme in the women's rights movement. Black women, queer women, people of color, and all groups who were shut out of the mainstream movements of feminism were either not invited or not talked about when we recount what happened in history.[17]

But the point is not to take this as a reason to shut that part of history out of our brains. The point is not to take that information as a reason to riddle ourselves with guilt and shame that we ignore the history or brush it off. We must acknowledge the context to learn why and how we went wrong and how and why we went right. Today, the notion of

---

15   Susan Milligan, "Stepping Through History: A timeline of women's rights from 1769 to the 2017 Women's March on Washington."

16   Joann M. Ross, "Making marital rape visible: A history of American legal and social movements criminalizing rape in marriage."

17   Tammy L. Brown, "Celebrate Women's Suffrage, but Don't Whitewash the Movement's Racism."

intersectional feminism continues to gradually grow, creating a movement for all women. That is a gradual and slow change that has arisen, and it comes both despite and because of times in the past. We have to continuously acknowledge the nuanced relationship that our modern-day has with its past, not demonize or glorify it.

If we pretend to be isolated generations, we ultimately harm ourselves by not learning from the past and not acknowledging how everything that is progress is a result of the work that was done by generations before us.

CONTEXT, CONTEXT, CONTEXT

I understand why we want to write off a lot of our history as just terrible things that terrible people did. As progressives who look at the world and see all the systematic problems that have been built up, we see that there are people just unequivocally praising this past, our instinct is to take the opposite side. To say, "No, there is nothing good about our history, our country sucks, our history sucks, and everyone was awful."

We come from a history of horrors. Columbus, slavery, Jim Crow, Japanese internment camps, the prison industrial systems…those are just some of our greatest hits. It's not surprising that people try to put history as a character of villainy. It's quite easy to do, considering the fright that took place. And it feels like the right thing to do! Certainly, a hell of a lot better than having statues and days dedicated to people who literally committed genocide (I'm looking at you, Columbus Day).

However, we have to understand that all those things were done by humans, humans like you and me, which means the terrible things that happened in the past could happen again.

Here's the awful truth: We are not naturally a better person than the person who owned a slave. We are not naturally better than the colonizers who came here and tortured and murdered Native Americans. And we are not naturally better than politicians who made the call for internment camps or the crime bill that led to our boom of prisons.

There was not some sort of evil DNA strain these people had that we don't have.

The person who owned slaves lived in a culture that was able to dehumanize an entire race. Yes, there were abolitionists and people who acknowledged the horror of slavery, but those individuals do not negate a system in our society that accepted and normalized it. Slavery was able to be engrained into the culture, and the desire that people have for power and capital was able to drown out qualms about what this was.

But still, instead of writing off slave owners or ostracizing places in the South as just naturally evil people and places, we have to look at the past and ask ourselves just *how* did that happen? Why and how does one become so obsessed with power that they can so easily torture, kill, rape, and punish for it? And in what ways do we see these kinds of behaviors manifest themselves in our generation?

If not, we end up with just different versions of the same toxic systems.

WHY DON'T WE LEARN FROM HISTORY?

We still see all the time a natural write off of things that we consider the "other." We see the dehumanization of groups and communities because it would be an inconvenience to our consciousness to humanize them.

To understand these things, we have to look back on our history and see these people as humans and these events as consequences of systems. We have to change our mental framework from a "cast of characters" to "complicated humans who existed in a different time."

I'm not trying to make the "it was a different time" excuse that is so typically used by our more conservative history defenders. But rather, looking at how that different time was allowed to exist where these terrible systems, movements, and people thrived; and how those toxic things have trickled down to our generation.

It's only through this framework that we explore how these systems have grown and changed and affected us. If we isolate generations and we isolate people and we isolate ourselves, then we never learn. We never learn and we always believe ourselves to be a hero of a solo story.

We think we are infallible because we know slavery is bad, and those people did not know slavery was bad. Therefore, they are evil humans who thankfully are dead and have made room for the people like you and me, the ones who are naturally good and fighting for good!

Dr. Geher spoke to me about all this. When I told him about how it seems like we group things in the past as "wholly good or bad," he explained why exactly we do that. "It's out-group homogeneity. Once you define something as an 'out-group' you begin to see them as 'all the same.'"

Hence, where issues of generation isolation and putting our history into narratives comes together to form the problem: We see the past as unrelated to us, and we view it as an out-group. And then because of this, we start to see these narratives become simpler and simpler. Good people and bad people. Easy to digest.

OUR HISTORY IS NUANCED AND COMPLICATED

Our generation is getting so much information all the time from so many different directions. In a study done by scholars from the Technical University of Berlin, the Technical University of Denmark, and other institutions, they examined our current attention spans, and the researchers "argue that the attention we can pay, as a society at large, is finite and getting zapped more quickly as we both take in more content and produce more ourselves."[18] With this, the instinct to put more things in our groups and simplify things to one homogenous view becomes not only appealing but also the easy and normal thing.

And this, as Dr. Geher said in our interview, leads to an "inability for people to interpret and appreciate nuance," and he made

---

18   Cassie Owens, "Our attention spans are shrinking. Here's why that matters."

it very clear that to push against this inability, takes active effort and the willingness and desire of the individual to do so.

Our history is not some mysterious thing of the past. We are our history; it lives in us and in our world as we evolve. If we don't begin to look at our history as something complicated and nuanced and appreciate it and criticize it for all that it was, our tomorrow won't look as good as it potentially could.

Think about our current moment from a historical perspective. I believe we got to where we are today because we didn't truly understand how our past still affects us. Huge populations of this country think we had entered a post-racial era in the wake of Barack Obama, leaving us vulnerable to the trappings of someone like Donald Trump gaining power and feeding into some deep sense of grievance and anxiety that America's future was leaving them behind, which then explicitly and more subtly encouraged more discriminatory behavior.

If we don't learn how to view our history through a lens of nuance and understanding, we'll never be able to see and appreciate how it creates who we are today. We won't progress into a world that is better; rather, we'll progress into another disjointed version of our history.

We cannot treat our history as just an isolated thing of the past. If we want to truly move forward and be better than our past, we have to acknowledge context for all the harm it caused and all the ways it was able to be a foundation for the good we see today. Change your mind.

CHAPTER 4

HISTORY IS NOT A STORY

———

Because we grow up surrounded by narratives in books, films, and television, it's no surprise we begin to see our own lives as narratives as well.

We try to paint it into everything: our history, our lives, ourselves. We take the seemingly random and dysfunctional facets that make up our world, and we try to put them into some sort of narrative sense. But what if this obsession of forcing story coherency on our lives is something that is ultimately getting in the way of our growth?

SO...IS OUR HISTORY A LIE?

I think many progressives can call back to a time where they learned or realized that a lot of the mainstream history that is either taught to us in class or through our culture is propaganda at best and straight-up lies at worst.

Look no further than our dear genocide committing, ocean sailing, Christopher Columbus.

I have a distinct memory of watching fun cartoons about Christopher Columbus and his discovery of the US in elementary school. My cartoon Columbus sang a song filled with rhymes about it being the year 1492 and the ocean being blue, he and his crew were jumping up and down with excitement when they found this new land, they traveled back to Spain to tell the royalty, and they were awarded big, animated jewels and coins. My cartoon Columbus was certainly not telling us about his genocidal tendencies.

In high school, I started to get a better understanding of the reality of our history. They taught us a bit about the truth, but it was certainly not an in-depth look. We got the genocide in Spark Notes addition, if you will; something light and quick, so when we went to the cafeteria for lunch after our history period, we could still stomach our food.

Once I got to college, it was not so much on the Spark Notes. One of my first classes my freshman year was regarding colonization. We read Columbus's journals, Edward Said's theory in *Orientalism, A Short Account of the Destruction of the Indies,* by Bartolomé de las Casa, watched documentaries on the subject, and also interpreted Shakespeare's *The Tempest* through the allegory of colonization.[19,20,21] Suffice it to say, we read as many texts as we could find recounting the history from the perspective of the Indigenous people. There were stories I read about the torture, the killing, the raping, the outright dehumanization, and heartless destruction that I will never forget.

---

19   Edward Said, *Orientalism.*
20   Bartolomé de las Casas, *A Short Account of the Destruction of the Indies.*
21   William Shakespeare, *The Tempest.*

I was not alone in being shaken by this, finally, more honest look at our history. Almost all my peers had a similar experience as I did when it came to learning about our past. We all recounted stories of the unique type of lie we each were told. Some of my classmates even talked about the ways that the story was taught to them, in which students had to "act out" the history. We talked about it for a whole class, each student confessing their version of whitewashed education, and the stories would range from culturally insensitive to outright bigotry.

But recently, there have been more and more efforts taken to combat the stories of Columbus that paint him as a hero. And although Columbus Day is recognized as a federal holiday, local governments and states can make the choice not to observe it. This has been happening more and more, with some places completely changing the name and purpose of the holiday from "Columbus Day" to "Indigenous People's Day."[22]

But none of that is enough. Maybe it's all those primitive years of learning about history through rose-colored glasses, or maybe it's the general culture that we exist in. Whatever it is, I think despite things like Indigenous Peoples' Day and the popularization of the idea that "maybe Columbus *wasn't* the hero," it still doesn't feel like it's clicking. It feels incredibly surface level and not as though there is any kind of deep understanding within any of us.

It's like I've become so accustomed to this as just the way the world is, I can't even reframe it to think about the past

---

22 Marilia Brocchetto and Emanuella Grinberg, "Quest to Change Columbus Day to Indigenous People's Day Sails Ahead."

correctly. And that scares me. We have to work to have a relationship with history that focuses on atonement beyond just surface level acts. And that means taking the time and making the effort to adjust your fundamental frameworks when it comes to our relationship with American history.

None of us can work to uproot dysfunctional colonial systems if we refuse to form a relationship with our history that acknowledges the reality of our past. We have to build frameworks that allow us to empathize in a way that acknowledges the discrepancies between communities that lead to populations being systematically disadvantaged aren't natural. And we have to allow this knowledge to spur us to take action toward reparations for the communities harmed in our histories' lies, without doing so by just having a framework of hating the country you live in.

IF IT'S SO BAD, WHY CAN'T WE JUST HATE OUR PAST?

It makes sense that people's reactions to learning about the history of our country can lead them to just take on the mantra of "well, fuck America." Because the country has such a distinct culture of patriotism and grandiose displays of the greatness of America, it's hard not to think the only way to combat that fairy tale is to have the polar opposite view.

This is especially true when you enter the realm of advocacy. You want to be a person who works to change the world. When you see something bad, you have to fight against it. Christopher Columbus is the villain, we are the hero, and to defeat him we have to hate him and teach about him as the villain he was.

So, while hating on the figures of the past who did bad things may seem like a radical and revolutionary take, ultimately, it's the easiest response, though not the best one

What is truly revolutionary is learning how to teach, process, and live with a nuanced version of history.

TEACHING HISTORY: WHO DOES HISTORY BELONG TO?

I became really fascinated with this idea of learning how to have a proper relationship with our history when I picked up *A People's History of the United States* by Howard Zinn. This book recounts history from the point of view of those who are not typically awarded a voice or the liberty of first-person perspective in mainstream's telling of history.

This book absolutely played a pivotal role in my own education on the reality of the United States. But beyond that, there was something I read in the introduction that struck me particularly in regard to how we teach history.

Anthony Arnove, who wrote the introduction, writes about Zinn, "Howard believed in laying his cards on the table. He did not hide behind the historian's easily available stance of distant, expert 'objectivity.' He had a point of view and was happy to be challenged and engaged in dialogue about it."[23] This idea of teaching about the perspective of the person who is distributing knowledge with honesty and who welcomes critical thinking rather than expecting automatic belief in what

---

23   Howard Zinn and Anthony Arnove, "Introduction to the Thirty-Fifth Anniversary Edition of a People's History of the United States," Introduction, in *A People's History of the United States*, xx.

they say really inspired me and made me do more research on Zinn himself and his ideologies behind the teaching of history.

Howard Zinn was a historian and most famous for his work in history and the influence that *A People's History* had. His entire life was defined by education. He was born to an immigrant Jewish family in Brooklyn, New York. He joined the Air Force in World War II, something that "helped shape his opposition to war and his strong belief in the importance of knowing history."[24] He was able to attend college under the GI Bill and worked through his schooling to receive a PhD. He was a professor at Spelman College in Atlanta, Georgia, during the Civil Rights movement, something he became very active in, and then worked at Boston University until he retired.

He wrote dozens of books and also founded the Zinn Education Project with a former student of his. This education project "is coordinated by two non-profit organizations, Rethinking Schools and Teaching for Change." Its goal is to "introduce students to a more accurate, complex, and engaging understanding of United States history than is found in traditional textbooks and curricula."[25]

I knew I wanted to speak to someone who was an expert on Zinn and his fundamental beliefs on teaching history from the perspective of those who didn't necessarily have the power. I found an article on the Zinn Project's website of someone defending *A People's History* and explaining their respect for Zinn.

---

24 "Biography," HowardZinn.org, September 15, 2020.
25 "Zinn Education Project."

The article was by a lifelong educator, and it was an incredibly interesting read. I decided to get in contact with that author and interview him about the manners through which we can teach and understand our very, very complicated history.

TEACHING HISTORY: THERE'S NO RIGHT ANSWER

Dr. Mark Kissling is a Professor of Education in the Department of Curriculum and Instruction at Penn State University. In our interview, he highlighted some of the important things that he keeps in mind as an educator, especially when it comes to teaching history.

"You have to teach with the acknowledgment of the positions of those writing," he said. "Our history is written by people in positions of power. They are the ones recording what's happening, so we know immediately that our history is recorded, known, and retaught to serve the interests of those in power."

"And as we exist as a society structured by supremacy and oppression and injustice, those in power benefit from that structure and benefit from upholding that structure to keep power."

Dr. Kissling highlighted the important concept of "what is your position," something I discussed in the previous chapter in relation to our position as individuals. But positionality relates to all things, and when something is masquerading as a "factual accounting of history," it is particularly important to remember how everything, as well as everyone in this world, comes from a unique perspective based on their position. This includes our history.

Often, our history is told from the dominant groups, who also happen to be the oppressors in a society that is based on supremacy. This explanation is different and more truthful than just saying, "Christopher Columbus was a monster."

Exploring the positionality of the figures of history allows us to see how society was structured in a way that allowed a man to become such a monster when given the opportunity for power. It allows us to explore how truly complex a person is without putting the blame on just "one man."

This changes our framework from blind hatred of our past to understanding it, critiquing it, and ultimately learning from it.

I asked Dr. Kissling about being an educator and how it feels to be the person relaying this kind of difficult information. We spoke about the particular importance of admitting biases and acknowledging positionality when in the office of educating.

"Many people seem to be afraid that it might weaken your teachings if you admit your biases, but it doesn't legitimize any of your knowledge to admit the biases you may have based on your own education and formations of thought," Dr. Kissling said.

He explained the complexity of admitting your bias. "When you do this, you take something that is abstract that is just accepted as norm and truth and complicates it." And as discussed in the previous chapter, it can be hard for us to choose to focus on a complicated thing when a simple answer is offered to us as such an appealing truth.

But admitting bias is the way to break away from teaching history that perpetuates systems of oppression.

"Powerful people and powerful institutions can never place themselves outside of the reality of positionality. That's when things become dangerous and oppressive because those who are in power can create a false narrative that their story is not 'their perspective,' but rather, the 'only perspective,'" Dr. Kissling said.

We have to expand our acceptance of what history is, who can teach it, and how to teach it. The entire notion of how we educate and how we formulate conclusions on our history could bear some reexamining.

Society shouldn't just be made up of older people teaching stories of the past to younger people. "We should teach from all angles," Dr. Kissling pointed out. "Educators and the country should listen and engage in real conversation with students and the youth. Society is not just the wisdom of elders but also the wisdom of youth."

Kissling went on to talk about how to critique and how conversations on things from different perspectives should be encouraged. History and the past should be seen as an open dialogue, not a rigid story with one perspective on what happened being fed as the truth.

"Debate and conversation should be encouraged. Not someone stating an opposing opinion just for the sake of it, but if someone has a different perspective, they should feel welcome to share it if it's based in real critical thought. You don't need to agree with me, but you do need to be able to argue with me."

The argument should not be demonized, and the purpose behind a debate should not be necessarily "to win." It's to engage in conversation and be open to real active listening and genuine dialogue between rational people, no matter their difference in life experience, perspective, age, race, or any of it.

We have to question the things in our history we just view as unequivocally true, and we have to reexamine the whole idea of "truth." This notion that there is "one reality" that some people know, and others don't just isn't possible because there is no one truth. There is no "one" narrative because we are all different people experiencing the world in different ways.

As Dr. Kissling said, "Take something that is abstract that is just accepted as norm and truth and complicate it."

We must seek to have frameworks that approach our history and our past with more openness and critical thinking. We must view history as something we seek to analyze and form possible conclusions from rather than as something that is one holistic truth.

Expanding our idea of what history is and who has a say in it, understanding positionality, and acknowledging biases does not weaken our history. It just changes the way we view it from a false narrative of one true tale, to looking at it constantly with a critical lens; not just learning history, but examining, interpreting, and critiquing it.

Dr. Kissling pointed out that to view it this way actually plays into the hand of the oppressive systems. He explained to me the difference between education and schooling:

> Schooling is an instrument of the power that is used to keep the masses in line; it is done to you. Education is not done to people; rather, it's people learning to live out their curiosity and being encouraged to exercise thought and action for those curiosities. You are not educated because some educator comes in, taps you on the shoulder, gives you knowledge, and declares you enlightened. Education is a constant critical engagement of the world around you.

This idea of reframing how we view our history and engaging in critique of our past is not reserved for the classroom. It's something we need to carry with us as we engage with the multiple facets of our culture that relate to our past.

TEACHING HISTORY: CRITICAL THINKING

I asked Dr. Kissling specifically about my theory of this human obsession with narrative coherence and simple answers, as well as the desire we have to shove our history into a costume of valor and bravery or villainy and horror. I asked if he found it hard, as an educator, to get people to understand history through a lens of humanity rather than simplicity.

"Complexity does not deny us of our humanity," Kissling said. I agree with him. In fact, I believe that the complexity is what ultimately awards us the best parts of our humanity.

History should not be taught through praise of one story and criticism of another, but rather a holistic critique of every affair.

And the way to push for that is to not only acknowledge it within ourselves, but also to fight and make sure to teach our history through the critical eye. We should push to teach and think about our past through the lens of critique. "And we have to make sure we acknowledge the difference between criticism and critique," Dr. Kissling added. "When I say history should be taught as a critique, I mean that we are constantly staying open-minded about it and actively thinking about it."

We have to embrace, as a framework for our lives, that complexity is our humanity. Denying it is to deny who we were, who we are, and who we want to be in the future.

IF THERE ARE NO VILLAINS, THERE ARE NO HEROES
Our obsession with casting the things in our past as either holistic villains or heroes oversimplifies everything and waters down humanity out of our figures of the past, leaving them as outlines of themselves that we common folk fill in as "good" or "bad."

It's as if we have a scale which we put a historic figure on, and if it tips more on the scale toward "good action," well, boom! we've got ourselves a historical hero, folks! But if it tips toward the bad...then watch out! We just cast the character of the villain, the person that is the reason why everything that's bad about our history and our present exists.

I'm currently reading a book about the US presidents. It's called *Don't Know Much About the American Presidents,* by Kenneth C. Davis. And the book goes through a summary of all our presidents and gives them a grade at the end. And you know what the reality is of the administrations of even the most historically legendary men that we put up on this pedestal?

Scandals. Corruption. Bankruptcies. In-fighting. Polarization.

All the stuff that we see today was happening to them. We all know that the first twenty presidents were either slave-owners or slave-owners adjacent. But I've also been learning things such as: the genius Thomas Jefferson basically had zero concepts of what money was and died of an "enlarged prostate, bladder infections, pneumonia, and chronic diarrhea" while seriously in debt.[26]

Nothing like learning all that to quickly humanize our beloved commanders in chief.

But that's not what we think about when we look back on our history. We either see these larger-than-life figures who

---

26   Kenneth C. Davis, *Don't Know Much About the American Presidents,* 100.

were our founding fathers who wrote this sacred text, or, more recently on the progressive side, we see them as awful power-hungry people. And how does that help us? How do we learn from them; the great things they did as well as the terrible acts they committed?

It works the other way too! Look at someone like Martin Luther King, Jr. This is a man who empowered millions, was a leader of a movement, and changed our country and history.

However, according to published FBI documents, Dr. King also allegedly bore witness to a rape, took money from a member of the Communist party, and his philandering "was even more rampant than historians knew [...] King took part in group sex. [...] King may have fathered a child with one of his mistresses."[27]

Should that erase him from our history? Should that turn his status of a hero to a villain in our books? No. The problem that arises from finding out that a historical figure did something horrific is only a scandal and an inherent issue if you've been thinking of that person as a deity. As David Greenberg writes in an article analyzing the revelations on MLK, "Awareness of these qualities doesn't mean despising figures once held up as heroes. Rather, it gives us a more complete and nuanced picture of the people who shaped our world."[17]

Power comes from seeing them as humans. Using the example of the founding fathers, the power comes from the

---

27 David Greenberg. "How to Make Sense of the Shocking New MLK Documents."

strength and mental work to come to terms with the horrible state of our country that allowed men and women to own and torture and murder other men and women with zero repercussions, while working through how that was simultaneously the country that allowed human beings to put pen to paper and write foundational texts guided by this radical principle of freedom that we still live by.

OUR NEW HISTORY AND GOOD OLD PATRIOTISM

One of the final things Dr. Kissling and I discussed was whether it would be possible to exist in a country with a well-rounded view of history and still have patriotism be a core characteristic of being an American. I asked him, "Should we relinquish our obsession with this idea of patriotism?"

"We need to complicate patriotism, but not throw it out," Dr. Kissling said. "Questioning and inquiry is patriotic, and seeking betterment is patriotic. We should be teaching our patriotism as questions and a work in progress, not an unquestionable given."

Again, it's about working to accept the complexities and fighting for something that is better. That is done through critical thought on what is wrong and how can we better it for everyone. Advancement doesn't come from total love or total hate. It comes from a place of collective betterment and growth.

WHEN WE ARE HISTORY, HOW DO WE WANT TO BE REMEMBERED?

Think about it from the perspective that you will be this nation's history in ten years, in a hundred years, in five hundred years.... Do we want them to hate us because we will inevitably fail in one way or another for the future's progressive standards? Or do you want them to see us as a complicated country beginning to work at uprooting invisible systematic problems, confronting realities of climate change, and reworking the political system to root out corruption and those seeking power just for power?

Growth comes from critical thinking. Growth comes from deep understanding. Growth comes from looking at what happened back then that led to so much horror and trying to figure out why. We have to work to change our frameworks from history as our villains or our heroes.

So, in the history books that talk about us, our years, this generation, this time, who will we be? Will we be a cartoon that makes fake promises and tells stories of grandeur, or will the following generations see the ways in which we didn't do enough and mark us as unforgivable monsters? Or can we begin to change our minds and push for a different reality and relationship with our past?

Our history is not one of villains or heroes. It is a history of complex and flawed humans. Change your mind.

CHAPTER 5

NATION OF RACISTS AND ELITISTS

————

I've discussed in the previous chapters how we like to turn the world around us into digestible narratives. This need to oversimplify applies to these upcoming chapters about how we categorize our country and those who inhabit it and the disservice we do to one another and to progress itself if we don't work to change these frameworks.

We simplify because our brains can't process all the information we receive in our lives. But often we let dangerous simplifications become our truth because they're easier to understand than a nuanced perspective.

In the case of our country, a massive place with over three hundred million people, we like to boil people down to just a simple label rather than trying to, you know…ingest the complexity of fifty states, thousands upon thousands of cities, or hundreds of millions of people.

That makes sense. Like I've said, our individual brains aren't equipped to grapple with the reality of millions of different lives and perspectives and contexts of one another's worlds. But what we often do in the place of that is lump together groups of people depending on where they're from in the US and associate stereotypes to these regions that can have dangerous repercussions in quests for progress.

I like to break down the US into four regions: West Coast, Midwest, South, and Northeast. Or, as we like to see it in our brains that prefer the effortless thought process: the California Land, the Whatever Area, the Racist Places, and the Home of the Elitists.

Obviously, that breakdown of a country and people in regions of a country can lead to some problems.

I HATE THE SOUTH...RIGHT?

I was born in Montreal, a city in Canada. I lived there until I was four years old when my family and I moved to Atlanta, Georgia, for my dad's job. I lived in Atlanta for fourteen years and actually went to the same school for all of it. The school my parents chose for us to attend was an international school, picked specifically because they wanted my sister and me to keep our French and wanted us to be surrounded by "global citizens." And that kind of did happen. The school was inhabited by plenty of kids from Atlanta and kids who grew up in the south, but a large majority either were from a different part of the US or from a different country. It was a great experience that gave me more global awareness, but it didn't exactly make me feel very connected to Atlanta or Southern culture while I was in school.

Growing up, I wanted so badly to move to New York. I would tell my mom that I was bored in Atlanta and that there was nothing to do. There were no cool people. Places like New York were in my movies and my TV shows and my books. Avengers headquarters? New York. The irrationally sized apartments and unrealistic amount of time in coffee shops of *Friends*? New York. *When Harry Met Sally*, *30 Rock*, and even the puppets of *Sesame Street* were living on a fictional street in real New York.

All the coolest stories happened in New York. All the coolest protagonists came from New York. I just wanted to be in a big city that wasn't in the middle of the terrible, hot South.

As I got older, I became less blindly enamored with New York. But I did become very attached to places similar to it. I became very devoted to the idea that my personality simply did not match my experience of the South. The stereotypical charming and welcoming and almost "fake" temperament of the South wasn't something I found to be as appealing as the suave, slightly rude stereotypes of those in Northern cities.

I didn't like that I was living in a state with such grotesque history. When we would go on field trips and left the perimeter of Atlanta, we would always see a confederate flag. I didn't like the fact that when the family visited, we would go out and do some tourist attraction activities, and one of those activities included walking up Stone Mountain. Stone mountain is, essentially, a massive rock (hence, the name) with an etching of confederate soldiers on the side.

All of this is to say, I didn't exactly claim the South with pride.

Not to mention, it felt correct to disown the South. Saying you were prideful of being from there essentially felt like saying you were okay with living around, or worse, being, a racist, a sexist, a homophobe…and obviously, that is never where you want to be when you consider yourself to be a person of the twenty-first century.

I remember distinctly when I was looking with a college counselor at my list of preferred schools. She looked up from my list and said,

"These are all in the Northeast."

"Yes," I had responded, sitting up straighter.

"But why?"

"I'm not staying here," I said laughing. "I'm not from here. You know? There's not exactly my people naturally in this area."

And that was that.

It was never mentioned again, and I never thought about it again as I finished out my senior year and graduated from high school. I lived in Atlanta because we moved here for my dad's job. I loved my friends, I loved my school, and I loved my experience growing up in Atlanta. But I certainly didn't love the city, much less the state or the entire region of the South. I was never going to stay past my graduation date.

"THE COUNTRY WOULD BE BETTER WITHOUT YOU"

Stereotyping the South is a mindset I easily fell into, and one that so many others have fallen into as well. The entirety of the South often feels like it is defined by racist stereotypes. But, just like viewing this country as a natural binary, this idea that one area of the country is bad while another is good is ultimately a complete falsehood. It's a narrative we use to help simplify our understanding of the holistic image of our country. But in order to achieve true progress, we must learn to investigate and change this mindset. We must complicate our view of the country and the people in different areas of this country.

Clearly, the previous stories of my view of the South are an indication that I had to come to understand this through experiencing the toxic mindset. And not until I actually went to the school in the Northeast, far, far away from the South as I had been so excited to do, did I realize there was a problem.

I went to school in Boston and everything changed. My view of this country was very modified, and my perspective of what it means to be progressive or conservative was transformed.

I noticed immediate differences walking the busy streets of Boston. I received fewer smiles from strangers, didn't make any pleasant eye contact with fellow Bostonians, felt an over-all lack of contentment, and almost never bore witness to any joyful interactions between strangers. Even if the weather was beautiful and perfect, it felt like the entire city was in a collective worse mood in Boston than in Atlanta. It should also be mentioned that these two cities' breakdown and demographics are also strikingly disparate.

Living in both of these cities, the difference is palpable.

One time in class I mentioned that I live in Georgia. This boy said with a smirk and said, "If you guys seceded from the Union, the country would be a better place." This was followed by a few nodding heads and chuckles.

That was definitely a jarring thing to hear. It's this kind of elitism and complete ignorance of what makes up Southern states that is so incredibly shocking when you move from the South to the North.

I started to realize that the "utopian life" I always thought existed in cities in the Northeast was a pipe dream. I started to realize the old views I had of my home state were also held by quite a few folks around me in Boston. And it started to become very jarring to hear people insult a place they had never been to before. I started to realize just how infuriating and unworthy the South was of the condescension that I had previously held and saw around me feel.

I'm sure when the boy in my class made that comment, he saw the secession of the South as ridding that part of the country that is more conservative, where much of our most shameful history took place. He thought he was making a valid point, even maybe a liberal one.

But do you also get rid of the barista who talks to me every time I get coffee at Starbucks? Who remembers me from high school and remembers where my friends all went to college? Does that mean getting rid of my stepfamily who have grown up in the South; who, in a time when their father was dying of brain cancer, had an entire community step up and help raise the kids who had lost a parent? Does that mean getting rid of the cities where a lot of the culture that has taken over this entire country was born? Or getting rid of the place that birthed the Civil Rights movement?

There are real people behind our stereotypes. There are stories behind the generalizations. And too often, we make "being progressive" a natural morality thing—something possible for certain types of people, but not others.

There are people and families who don't have the time to be plugged into the news twenty-four seven; who aren't raised in schooling systems that teach about prejudice or the complex realities of our history; who don't have money for an education that will teach them about the pitfalls or benefits of capitalism and show them various philosophical theories of how to exist in our society.

Are these individuals to blame for the issues in our country? Do we really believe that by virtue of their limited views of the world and the fact that they live in the South, the mecca of racism, that they should no longer be a part of our nation?

There is no doubt and no denying the fact that abhorrent things have occurred in the South. It's home to not only some of the most discriminatory individuals but also legislations, communities, and cultures that are far less open-minded and more conservative than you see in many other places in the country. But viewing individuals as the fault for a systematic issue is not an acceptable or effective framework.

I'm not pretending like people's stereotype of the South is unfounded or nonsensical. I'm just saying there's far more to the South than these aspects, far more than the stereotypes and the groupings.

In addition, the issues of the South are not some sort of isolated incident. We are one country. If there is an issue of racism and bigotry and supremacy, it is not coming only "from one place," and, therefore, we cannot solve the issue by "getting rid of that place" or even if the South gets its act together.

No one is exempt from the criticisms of this country. Nothing makes one individual outside the realm of the problem, not education or family or home state. No one is absolved from the issues. Everyone needs to be part of the solution.

Another thing has become particularly important to mention, especially in the wake of election results, is that if it's not disdain for the South then it's outright just dismissal of its existence. I was talking about it with my stepfamily, who were all raised in Georgia. I said, "I never realized it, but it's like I grew always up thinking about them, you know? Everyone always talked about how cool New York and Boston are, and you just are generally so aware of the states and the world in the northeast. But it honestly feels like they grew up and didn't even spare us another thought."

"Yup. They're in our world, but we're not a part of theirs," my stepmom, Catherine, responded with a chuckle.

This became even more apparent after this most recent election. Georgia went blue in the general and also held runoffs with results that determined Democratic control of the US Senate. The general narrative had never been that Georgia could elect a Democrat once, let alone twice, and forget about three times! The way that people who weren't from the South were floored by the election results made it obvious that when they were drawing out their maps and figuring out who had to win to keep control of the Presidency, the House, and the Senate, Georgia, most certainly, had not been on their minds.

And this surprise, this feeling that progressives around this country were turning their eyes on the South for the first time because now it served their interest, was honestly hurtful and infuriating. And it's one of the clearest showcases of the detriments of having a framework that allows you to erase regions of this country because you deign them and all within them "the conservative folks." You miss the organizing that's happening on the ground. You miss the fight that real people are doing day in and day out to get the right people elected and change the institutions that allow the oppressive systems to dominate in the South.

People have to start changing their frameworks on how they view this part of the country so they're not caught so off-guard next time this kind of thing happens, and they can participate or be aware of the work done to overturn injustices and help transform this entire county. And no, posting a picture of Stacey Abrams on social media is not enough.

These are systematic problems we are working to change. It's everyone's problem and everyone's responsibility, but it's no one's fault. When we spend all of our time blaming each other and looking for something to hate for what's going on today, we never look forward to tomorrow.

BEING FROM THE NORTHEAST

Okay, so I knew that my perspective of the Northeast was very biased and not well-rounded. The Northeast is the place that helped me open my eyes to the reality that this country as a whole is messed up, and it opened my eyes to the beauties I had been missing in my views of where I grew up. As such, in direct opposition to the ideas I am writing about, my view of the Northeast went from utopic, fun, liberal city to a hellhole that is ignorant and elitist.

So, to get a more well-rounded understanding (and to stop being a horrible hypocrite), I wanted to hear from someone who had grown up in the Northeast to understand what it's like; to be from the place where the stereotype is "you're from the place with all the elitists" rather than "you're from the place with all the racists."

I spoke to a friend of mine from college. He grew up in Massachusetts, and he thought he would spend his college years in DC. He spent his freshman year at American University but transferred to Emerson College in Boston for multiple reasons. He's a performing arts major, and the program (and financial aid) was better at Emerson. But most importantly, he also wanted to be closer to his home.

"When you live here it gets pretty funny to hear what everyone thinks because you hear all these stories of how Mass is such a liberal place. Sometimes people are criticizing, but mostly they're complimenting how amazing and liberal it is," Carl said. "But if you live here, especially if you have lived basically anywhere in Massachusetts other than Boston, you know that isn't true. There are so many conservatives. Like, there is much of the Northeast that is not filled with elitist people who work in the city. There's a whole lot of hick-town."

And while I would advise the general population to move away from terms like "hick-town," the point Carl is making is that, again, there's more than meets the eye everywhere— for everyone.

He spoke to me about his vision of people from certain areas of the country before going to college. "Honestly, before college, I'm not even fully sure I knew what the Midwest was. I didn't really think about the area or the people one way or another. And now I've met a bunch of them from there, and I love them. They're just, you know, kind people. As for the South…it was just cowboy boots and a funny accent for me for many years. I think when I thought of the South I was only ever thinking about Texas, and I just thought of it as a place of Republicans and conservatives. College has changed that sweeping generalization, but yeah, that's what I used to think."

My evidence here is undeniably anecdotal. However, speaking to Carl and experiencing college and having lived and been in multiple different regions of our country, there is no denying that we are quicker to view the places that we don't come from as the "other." Stereotype, categorize, simplify.

But at what cost to progress?

WHY DO WE DO IT?

Brian Resnick, journalist and current senior reporter at Vox, wrote an article for *The Atlantic* in 2011 asking the million-dollar question: "The American Idea: Why Do We Hate Each Other?"

In that inquiry, Resnick explores answers to the root of hatred, to the root of much of what I'm talking about in this book: the polarization, the simplification, the black and white reactionary thinking.

Resnick analyzes an essay written by Francis Edward Clark in 1921 exploring this very subject. In the article and in the essay, both men write about how it comes down to our own insecurities. It derives from this fear we have within our in-groups to reach out to others because the only way that outreach is successful is if the people in the out-group are also willing to reach out to you.

It's a matter of trust. It's also a power dynamic. We have to adjust our mindset from "if I reach out to this other group, they're going to steal the power that I have and that I have accumulated from viewing myself as better than them" to "if I reach out to this group, we both gain more power due to our decision to trust each other rather than constantly trying to undermine one another or use the other to prop ourselves up."[28]

This is the issue of power. We are so convinced it's finite that it seeps into everything. People are so afraid to lose power and so desperate to gain it. This thinking has led our country to this toxic way of constantly viewing things that we consider "the other" as inferior. We're not evil for doing so. We're not bad people. It's a psychological instinct.

And for the advancement of our country, we need to fight this instinct. We need to make sure that our solution is not to simply ignore the parts of the country we don't understand or have never experienced. We must reframe our thinking to understand that real power in trying to make this country better should never derive from putting others down.

Understand the instinct we have for in-groups and resource hoarding, especially when it comes to things like power and access to capital and fight that way of thinking. Make an active effort to change our mental framework of people and areas in this country, knowing that erasing people and places you might not understand or like is, in the end, effective only for people fighting our quest for progress.

SPLIT THE MAP IN TWO—IT'S ME VS. YOU!

Similar to what I was talking about in our natural mindset of black and white mentality leading to polarization, the argument of the South and the North is intrinsically connected

---

28 Brian Resnick, "The American Idea: Why Do We Hate Each Other?"

to these divisions. Jason Sokol, American historian, professor, and author, examines how these direct comparisons boil down these areas to cheap stereotypes or easy labels and how the South and the North see one another as simply the "other." In his book, *All Eyes Are Upon Us: Race and Politics from Boston to Brooklyn*, Sokol writes:

> *Twenty-first-century political maps paint the regions in red and blue, signifying two worlds at war inside one national soul. To many northerners, the South still feels foreign marked by its politics, culture, and race relations, even its weather and its food. In turn, many southerners hold fast to their regional identity, separating themselves from elitist liberals up north. Comparisons inevitably begin with prominent touchstones: Union against Confederacy, snow versus sun, New England foliage juxtaposed against Mississippi magnolias, Vermont maple syrup, and Georgia pecan pie. Southerners, in twangs or drawls, still boast about life's easier rhythms and slower pace. Northerners, through hard Boston accents or the coarse cadences of Brooklyn, continue to think of their environs as the hub of the universe; the South stands as retrograde or inscrutable or both.[29]*

The argument of racism in the South versus the North is another hot topic issue. There was a social media post that went fairly viral during the height of the BLM movement, "You Are Not Better Than People In The South: A Response

---

29 Jason Sokol, "The North isn't better than the South: The real history of modern racism and segregation above the Mason-Dixon line."

to Regional Biases and 'Liberal Safe Haven' Elitism," by @thenamesO on twitter. According to her bio, this woman's first name is Odion, and she is a Black woman, born to Nigerian parents and raised in the South. She spoke about her experiences when she told people where she was from, similar to what I have heard, and my friends have heard: the pity and the stereotypes.[30]

Odion explains how this commentary shows this common belief that racism is exclusive to a regional area and allows people to feel exempt from any criticism. "Your negative perception of the South is harming us. The 'lost cause' trope prevents people from investing in us. The perpetuation of Southern stereotypes erases our plight and mocks our resiliency. Stop using the South as your scapegoat for racism, a cushion for your apathy, and shield from your own shortcomings."[31]

Racism is not regional. This is the same argument Howard Zinn made way back in 1964 in *The Southern Mystique*.[32] Zinn argued that the South's issues are the issues of the entire country, just less hidden than everywhere else.

> *The South is everything its revilers have charged, and more than its defenders have claimed. It is racist, violent, hypocritically pious, xenophobic, false in its elevation of women, nationalistic, conservative, and it harbors extreme poverty in the midst of ostentatious wealth. The only point I have to add is that the United*

---

30 @thenamesO, "YOU ARE NOT BETTER THAN PEOPLE IN THE SOUTH—THREAD!" Twitter, July 9, 2020.

31 Ibid.

32 Howard Zinn, *The Southern Mystique*, 262.

States, as a civilization, embodies all of those same qualities. That the South possesses them with more intensity simply makes it easier for the nation to pass off its characteristics to the South, leaving itself innocent and righteous.[26]

The problem of one part of this country is the problem of a country. We are one nation and ultimately one people. Pretending like the "good" belongs to some and the "bad" is to blame is a framework of thinking that does nothing to move us toward progress, and it is just plain wrong.

As we have become more polarized and our regional divides more enforced, we are migrating toward the people who agree with us, cementing these ideals as we surround ourselves in the comfort of an echo-chamber encouraged by our regional agreements. It does not push for the shift of mental frameworks that we absolutely must work for. It's more than just the stereotype of the cowboy in the South and debutant in the North. This is about whether we continue to enforce systematic problems that allow oppression and systems of inequity to be our drivers.

Our mental frameworks that accept cheap labels and easy explanations as reality will lead to more separation, more divides, and less of a collective effort to understand and dismantle the systematic problems of our country. We must change the way we think about each other and our country if we have any hope at all.

SO WHO'S FAULT IS IT?

We view one another as just lump wholes, give those groups one identity, and call it a day. This grouping and pushing of entire geographical regions and those who inhabit it as part of an out-group means we run the risk of associating everyone in those areas as "bad" and "not like us."

It seems like in the progressive world we have an understanding of the issue: our problems are systematic. There is general consensus of this fact that is rooted deep in our culture. And yet, how can we expect to deal with fundamental systematic issues that reach across the whole country when we view people who aren't from where we are as part of an "out-group?"

If we plan to see progress and create change, it will not be with only "certain people" who come from "certain places." Issues will not resolve once we all agree that the South is Hell and the Northeast is Heaven. Both are places with complexity and culture. And despite what the history of either region is, despite the stereotypes that we associate with these regions, we cannot associate these generalizations to the individuals who inhabit these places.

We don't progress by blaming individuals for systems of oppression. This makes space for unceasing internal conflict and urges us backward, not forward.

THE GOAL OF OUR ADVOCACY SHOULD NOT BE HOMOGENEITY

The issue is that we start at judgment, stereotypes, and inferiority or superiority complexes, and we go from there. It relates to the things I have spoken about already. We crave simplicity. We have such strong desires to be part of the in-group that we will belittle all those around us to prop ourselves up. This happens everywhere all the time. I am speaking broadly right now, but I know for a fact that people, culture, and life is vastly different in Texas than it is in Georgia.

I grew up in Atlanta, but my dad lived in Snellville, Georgia, with my stepfamily. The distance between my mom and dad's house was only thirty-five minutes, an hour tops if it's Friday at five o'clock. Yet, the two places are quite different. One has tall buildings and a busy, hectic city life. Atlanta is famous for its cultural influence, and you can feel that pride within the city limits. Snellville is suburban life with spread out stores and outlet malls and where sometimes it feels like the most exciting thing to do is drive-through takeout. It is two different worlds that sit thirty miles away from one another.

But the point is not to understand the behaviors and cultures and individual identities of every single corner of this country. The point is not to ignore or look down on what we don't understand or haven't experienced.

We will never understand every crevice and corner and street and city in this country. But we can learn to appreciate the fact that the country is made up of so many tiny different facets.

That's what makes our nation so unique: its size and its diversity. We do not want to be people who think and act the same. Ignoring the reality of the makeup of this country, pushing areas of the country and its people into boxes, does nothing for true advancement.

When we lean into these ideas and stereotypes, we do what we do best: We comfort ourselves with narratives of simplicity. We view parts of this country as separate worlds from other parts. And we allow this to become the reality more and more because we use these stereotypes to completely detach ourselves from the places that we see as different from us and the beliefs of where we come from.

But we have to fight these instincts. We have to work to transform these frameworks and stop accepting them as simply a harmless norm. Because we know that's not the truth and that they, in fact, cause great harm. And if we spend our time attempting to solve the issue by finding something at fault, we have moved in no way closer to a better future.

No region is to blame. The system, which includes everywhere and all of us, is to blame. Change your mind.

CHAPTER 6

ACKNOWLEDGING THE WHOLE COUNTRY

———

"Fly-over country," "the heartland," "the prairie"—all things we've called that massive region in our country that sort of just...isn't really acknowledged or thought about by those who don't live there: the elusive Midwest.

Another word that is often associated with the people in the Midwest is "silent majority." As much as we may try to ignore this part of the country or pretend like it's just miles of empty land with no people to be found, it's not the truth.

If our efforts to make this country a better place don't include everyone, from the people on the most populated and popular coasts to those who live in agricultural regions with town centers populated with only a few hundred, are we really seeking something that is better for all, just for the few—or just for those with a lived experience that resembles our own?

WHAT IS A "MIDWEST?"

If you're not from the Midwest, it feels in some ways like it doesn't exist. When I mentioned that I was writing about the area to my friends from the urban South or Northeast I would get statements like, "Who even lives there," "they're just white trash of this country," and "imagine actually living there." I'm not saying that from a place of judgment. In fact, I would be the first one to make a joke just like a few years ago.

These stereotypes are normally given and exacerbated by those with no experience with the Midwest. If you have no affiliation with this broad region of the country, how often do you think about the states in this area, save maybe when we're in a general election?

My sister went to Kenyon College in Ohio. I used to question why in the world my sister went to a school surrounded by more cornfields than the human population. Why would she want to go to school so far away from us? Why would she want to go to school so far away from people who grew up like us and think like us? The worst part wasn't that I didn't understand how that might appeal to her, however. The problem was that I judged her for wanting to be there at all.

My view of the Midwest was not inherently negative in the same way I've seen many perceptions of the South. It wasn't a false ideal of elitism like I've seen of the North. It wasn't a view of unrealistic idealism like we see in many perceptions of the West Coast. It's just not a part of the country I ever thought about, seen as just land filled with nothing in the middle of the country.

THE HUMANITY IN "FLYOVER COUNTRY"

I began to "humanize" these states and the people within them when I went to the Iowa Caucus in January of 2020. I spent five days going to rallies, eating at chain restaurants, going to political talks, and driving through many, many aforementioned fields of corn. And I had an incredible time and met some wonderful people.

If all you know about the Iowa Caucus is that it's a dated and strange step on the road to elections, you might not know that one of the staples of the caucus is that the people of Iowa take it *very* seriously. They know that it's one of the only times where the country is really watching them. They know it's one of the only times where they, as citizens of a state in the Midwest, will do something that will affect the rest of the country, and as such, they will actually be taken seriously by the rest of the country.

So, when going to rallies for Bernie Sanders, I would bump into someone I had stood in line with at a Pete Buttigieg event or pass someone in the bathroom who I had seen at the Andrew Yang Q&A. They went to all the events because they wanted to have a real and full understanding of what each candidate represented. They wanted to hear, firsthand, what these candidates were going to do and say to earn their vote.

It is true that they were just a bunch of white people disconnected from progressive and "correct" thought as framed by urban leaders. They were just humans living their lives, wanting to examine each candidate to find out who will make sure they can afford to send their kid to college; who will make sure they won't lose their jobs; who will genuinely think about them and their home states in their administration and not just during an election season.

They did not look down on us students. Despite the fact we may have looked like strange trespassers or Northeast observers, the Iowans didn't treat us like that. They weren't mad at us for taking up space in line. Instead, they joked with us about how it was simply unacceptable how hot it was considering it was January in Iowa. We stood laughing and sweating outside a high school gym, standing in line for a Pete Buttigieg rally in boots, long sleeves, and jeans.

When I drove from rally to rally, I realized that stretches of fields without civilization for miles can be incredibly beautiful. Staring out the window and looking at these parts of the country untainted by the footsteps of bustling people with stretches of grass and snow and land that went so far beyond what the eye could see. It made this observer grapple with the realization of just how much the Earth outgrows and outweighs the people in it.

As philosophical as it may seem, I started to think about the inherently selfish nature of only thinking or respecting places in this country that are filled wall to wall with bodies and people and casting aside places that are made up more by the natural creations of the environment. Yes, the Midwest is far larger and less populated than other regions in our country. However, why should that matter?

Emptiness, lack of people, smaller city, and a less mainstream contemporary culture should make us acknowledge something as different, not as obsolete.

BEING FROM THE MIDWEST

To get a better understanding of what it really means to be from the Midwest—to experience what it means to live in the United States as a person from this area—I wanted to talk to someone who had experienced this world beyond a four-day political weekend getaway.

I spoke to Lilly, a friend of mine from college. She's from Illinois, living a few hours from Chicago (i.e., one of the few cities in the area that the rest of the country acknowledges). She also went to the Iowa Caucus and had a good time laughing at our expense as we discovered all the novelties of her home region.

I asked Lilly how she thinks the rest of the country sees the Midwest, and how does that perception actually fare from the real thing?

"I believe the rest of the country views the Midwest itself as a bunch of cornfields and the people that live there as polite, but not much more," Lilly said. She added on the feeling of erasure and how that leads to vast misconceptions. "Sometimes, I even think that people who aren't from the Midwest forget that it exists. But in reality, the Midwest is not really different than any other parts of the country. It's true that there is a lot of agriculture, but the Midwest also has big cities, which are innovation hubs and have their own culture, just like everywhere else."

I also asked Lilly about generalizations the Midwest makes about the rest of the country:

"You know, it's interesting," she said. "A generalization in the Midwest is that if you live here, you'll stay here. The student from a Midwest high school goes to a midwestern college and lives in a midwestern state after that. As someone who chose to go to college in the Northeast, I felt like the response, not necessarily from my peers but from older family members, was a bit of confusion as to why I would leave. It is assumed in the Midwest that if you are going to the East Coast, you're looking for a successful career. Other regions have other stereotypes. The South is racist, and the West Coast is where the pretty, fake, rich people live."

I know that stereotypes exist about all of us all across the country. But something Lilly said in the interview stuck out to me: "People are surprised you want to leave." I was genuinely shocked. Especially with the association that going to the Northeast meant "seeking success," people still don't understand why anyone would want to leave the Midwest. That kind of thinking is just foreign to me.

Of course, it is ridiculous that should surprise me. These are people's homes, their upbringing, surrounded by people who are familiar to them and who understand them. But I saw it as a stretch of field, and that's it.

Everything that Lilly shared seems obvious. The Midwest is home to so many people. There are families, industries, and all the human things that make up this area. And yet, I still saw it as "the empty land of farmers who elected Trump." Why is that?

When I was talking with Lilly about the harm these assumptions may have, she said, "I do think the regional culture has some role in shaping us, but it absolutely does not define us."

She experienced the exact same thing I'm talking about regarding stereotypes of the Midwest for the rest of the country. "It wasn't until I went to college that I realized the assumptions I'd been making all my life about other places in the country were not true at all. Any type of person can be found anywhere in the country," she said.

And she's right. When we shove people into categories, it's always harmful. And we talk about that a lot. We talk about the harms of racial stereotyping people and how that harms the communities as well as the society as a whole.

But I don't think we spend nearly enough time talking about the groupings and stereotypes we do as a collective about *massive* regions of this country.

Why was my instinct to look at the Midwest and assume the worst of it or just blindly trust other stereotypes and jokes I've heard? Why do so many accept this mental framework that just erases whole parts of this country?

That is such an issue considering the fact that there is absolutely no way everyone will get the opportunity to go anywhere in the Midwest and even less of an opportunity to interact with so many locals as I did. And that's okay. The solution to this is certainly not getting everyone to travel to the places they've never been. There are so many parts of this country that I have never experienced and probably never will. But that shouldn't mean I need to look down on them or judge them or assume one thing or another.

It should not take firsthand experience for empathy. The effort to prioritize everyone's humanity should be the mental framework I work toward no matter my direct experience with these communities.

DEFENDING THE MIDWEST

Like everywhere else, the Midwest is home to many people. It's also a *massive* part of our country, central to many of our nation's job markets, cultures, and influence.

Patti Waldmeir wrote an article for *Financial Times* titled, "I Heart the Heartlands: In Defense of the US's Misunderstood Midwest." She's a journalist who grew up in Detroit and went to college at the University of Michigan, experiencing the first part of her life in the Midwest. She writes about that experience, saying, "Even as a child growing up in Detroit, I was aware that the rest of the country—not to mention the world—looked down on us Midwesterners."[33]

In the article, she describes the misconceptions and her difficulty of showcasing the nuance of the Midwest and detailing the real makeup and personality of this massive region of our country in her journalistic writings. She explains the particular difficulty when it comes to explaining her home

---

33 Patti Waldmeir, "I Heart the Heartlands: In Defense of the US's Misunderstood Midwest."

region of the country to the rest of the population and the world, saying, "As in every election, we will all—local reporters or coastal, Americans or foreigners—struggle mightily to capture that special Midwest essence without descending to caricature."

In the article, Waldmeir tries to dismantle common negative stereotypes associated with the Midwest like the serotype that the Midwest is all "flyover land." She points to some of the more beautiful scenery of these states and talks about the booming tech industry that employs millions of people. Waldmeir tries to paint a picture that captures the region as something more multifaceted than the common stereotypes.

Waldmeir explains that these stereotypes are not just harmful from a morality standpoint, but also harms us politically and in the fight for progress. Waldmeir writes that "these days we are faulted not just for being hicks—we're also held responsible for almost single-handedly ushering Donald Trump into the White House."

However, she is also quick to explain how that fault occurred, referencing a quote from Wayne Youngquist, a Wisconsin political analyst. Youngquist says that "when Hillary Clinton referred to Trump supporters as 'deplorable' [before the 2016 vote], I think that sealed the election right then." Waldmeir adds, "Wisconsin voters abhor being condescended to by the likes of Clinton, a born Midwesterner who abandoned the region to spend decades on the coast. They hate being sneered at. And while many factors, economic and sociological, can explain the rise of Trump, I agree with Youngquist that the biggest factor was this sneering."[27]

Waldmeir talks about the misconceptions that surround the heartlands. And she is not afraid to address how this can have real consequences. If we claim that "we are seeking progress for all, the betterment of the country as a whole," how can we expect people to believe us when we ignore, group, or condescend whole regions of the country?[28]

And the greatest of truths, I've come to realize, and the reason I'm writing this book, is that people don't need to see you in the Midwest declaring your love for each person or canvassing on important issues. You don't have to write dissertations on the complex humanity of the Midwest. You don't need to make dedicated social media posts about your openness to the people of the Midwest.

You certainly *can* do all of those things. But don't do so as a replacement for the internal work you need to do; the quiet mental work that only you really know about. It takes time and effort and choice to actively change the way your mind reacts and thinks of these places. And we should never negate the inherent power that comes solely from changing your mental frameworks when it comes to different parts of the country.

If we work to change our framework so you start to view all parts of this country as worthy, and we recognize that the progress we seek should be a thing that everyone deserves, then the change in our view of that part of the country and the citizens within has a much more powerful impact. It starts changing the condescending narrative, and it fights the in-group versus out-group instinct. It may not seem like a lot, but our individual choice to broaden our minds can have a massive affect.

PROGRESS MEANS PROGRESS FOR ALL OF US

I wanted to dedicate an entire chapter to the Midwest because, as a progressive, I feel as though this region is the most ignored of the entire country. Either "irrelevant farmers" or "idiot Trump supporters" live there, both things I've heard said in liberal spaces by people who consider themselves open-minded progressive people. I'm not saying that is everyone's mindset, and I'm not blaming anyone who's said or thought that in the past. Hell, I know for a fact that I have to actively stop those very thoughts when I'm frustrated about the state of our country, our electorate, or our politics, and I'm looking for something to blame.

But this movement can't just be for the people who are loudest and proudest and most obviously fit the bill of what it means to be a "leftist." It has to be for everybody, and that starts with changing our perceptions of who's to blame for issues and changing our framework of what it means to be a "progressive." If we are seeking to create real change, that means there has to be room at the table and in the conversation for everyone. That happens when we change how we think about people from other parts of the country.

If not, we have a movement for only a certain type of person, with only a certain type of lifestyle, and who are only from a certain type of place. That leads to us ignoring pockets of the country, and that's when we have real problems. Communities feel isolated, left out, become more extreme, and grow hateful toward groups they thought left them behind. Then where does that lead us? I think we've already seen what can happen, and it's the presidency of a reality TV star.

The casual dismissal of the Midwest can no longer be something that we do for a quick, easy, and cheap joke. When we're thinking about the country and the country's thinking, we can't think that everyone experiences the nation the same way in New York, Des Moines, or San Francisco. We have to work to change our minds from automatic dismissal of the Midwest because our stereotype of it doesn't fit into our narrative of a "progressive future."

We have to change our thinking to include them into the vision of the ideal future, not envision a future where we just hope people from the Midwest or people from the South just eventually "fall in line."

If our idea of a better country is truly better for everyone, then we have to start making that the core message: inclusivity over exclusivity.

Change your thinking to acknowledge people in places in this country that you haven't visited before. Start including them in your mission on systemic reform.

Ultimately, we are one nation. Our future is a better one when we understand this. We are advocates for every part of the country, not just those we understand and see as "progressive." There is horror and beauty everywhere in this country. But most importantly, there is potential. We advance when we look at the things we don't understand and seek to understand them. We advance when we push away our instinct of out-groups and in-groups or of one thing good and the other bad. When we appreciate the difference, we comprehend nuance.

Fragmentation and separation will only lead us to a distorted version of our nation. Understanding and empathy will make tomorrow a place that is truly better than what we see today. All of us advance or none of us do.

Progress can't just exist in cities; progress must be a nation-wide endeavor. Change your mind.

CHAPTER 7

OBSESSED WITH THE BINARY

Our country's obsession with the binary is like taking a multiple-choice test. If there's a question, "Yes or no: Do you think racism/homophobia/xenophobia/etc. is bad?" there's a group of people who would still answer no, and once they get their act together, we'll be on the right track. Unfortunately, it's not that simple, and having frameworks that prop up binary thinking leads us to think there's this good/bad, yes/no, either/or easy solution. But it's never that simple.

I've discussed our desire to oversimplify things and the dire need to accept nuance in the quest for progress. But I want to talk specifically about our tendency toward binary thinking and try to figure out why we are obsessed with life as a zero-sum game and can't accept things as their full complicated selves.

I started thinking about the concept of polarization through this general idea of the "obsession with a binary" after a class discussion on the limitations of the gender binary and how made up the whole concept is. In the introductory class for this course on gender, my professor put up the word "girl" and the word "boy" on the board and had us just throw out terms that we associated with those words. She then broke down how each word we gave was socially constructed. She explained how the entire idea of a thing being "girl-like" or "boy-like" was completely arbitrary and made up, done to preserve our cultural hegemony.

I had always known about these ideas in an abstract sense. But hearing the contrast with the word "binary" got me thinking about this notion of one thing or the other thing. Our obsession with it can be this or that, a or b, good or bad, black or white. We can see this play out in obvious examples, like gender roles or political parties, but it goes far beyond a few anecdotal examples. Binary thinking is something that has become completely entrenched in every facet of our society.

I know that even in my common day-to-day rhetoric, I say things like, "I hate men," or "everyone that goes to that school is racist." Or, if we know that someone once said something a bit problematic, my friends and I will comfortably say, "No, they're literally homophobic." This is fairly innocent behavior—teenagers just being lighthearted and over dramatic. But the rationale behind that thinking is rooted in something problematic.

Making these statements about someone's identity because they didn't do everything that completely aligned with my core beliefs exist in the category opposite of me. It's what pushes people away from one another and isolates us in our binary belief systems.

And just how harmful can it get when these ideas become so entrenched that, all of a sudden, everything around us has become black and white? You're this or you're that, you're good or you're bad, I hate you or I love you—how can that be sustainable for our country long term?

THE BINARY'S OUTCOME: POLARIZATION

Despite the general attachment the word "polarization" has to politics, it's actually, in the most basic of terms, a "division into two sharply distinct opposites." But that doesn't cover nearly enough of the minutiae of polarization.[34]

Polarization does not just mean we disagree with people, and my argument here is not that we need to evolve to a place where we no longer disagree with anyone, and we all hold hands and sing Kumbaya. Polarization is not disagreement. An article from *Greater Good Magazine* wrote, "Polarization occurs when we refuse to live next to a neighbor who doesn't share our politics, or when we won't send our children to a racially integrated school. The force that empowers polarization is tribalism: clustering ourselves into groups that compete against each other in a zero-sum game where negotiation and compromise are perceived as betrayal, whether those groups are political, racial, economic, religious, gender, or generational."[35]

---

34 *Merriam-Webster.com Dictionary*, s.v. "polarization."
35 Zaid Jilani and Jeremy Adam Smith, "What Is the True Cost of Polarization in America?"

Merriam-Webster's definition of polarization follows up the simpler six-word definition above by saying that polarization occurs especially when it is in "a state in which the opinions, beliefs, or interests of a group or society no longer range along a continuum but become concentrated at opposing extremes." And it's in this part of the definition that we begin to see how polarization leads to something truly horrifying. [29]

"Concentrated at opposing extremes"—this leads to an extremely polarized environment. We already view the other side as inferior in character. A "2016 Pew polling found that 47 percent of Republicans said that Democrats are more 'immoral' than other Americans; 35 percent of Democrats held that view about Republicans."[36] But the polarization also might force us to think that we can't even outwardly disagree with the group we've identified with.

In the article written by Zaid Jilani and Jeremy Adam Smith, they quote a study done by three political scientists at Dartmouth, "The Nature and Origins of Misperceptions." Smith and Jilani write that these "three political scientists note that in polarized situations we feel intense 'social pressure to think and act in ways that are consistent with important group identities.' Instead of thinking for ourselves, we tend to reason 'toward conclusions that reinforce existing loyalties rather than conclusions that objective observers might deem 'correct.'"[37]

---

36 Ibid.

37 D.J. Flynn, Brendan Nyhan, and Jason Reifler, "The Nature and Origins of Misperceptions: Understanding False and Unsupported Beliefs About Politics."

Binary thinking leads to polarization, which then leads to strict in-groups and out-groups, something that Dr. Geher touched on briefly in our interview. But to delve into more detail, this kind of grouping is a part of psychology's social identity theory, which proposes that "the groups (e.g., social class, family, football team, etc.) which people belonged to were an important source of pride and self-esteem. Groups give us a sense of social identity: a sense of belonging to." This theory functions under the fundamental belief that we are always grouping members of society, and the only manner you can find identity in your group is through understanding you aren't part of that "other group."[38]

Because your in-group essentially only survives through the belief that there is an out-group, "the central hypothesis of social identity theory is that group members of an in-group will seek to find negative aspects of an out-group, thus enhancing their self-image."

So, it is not very surprising people spend time degrading those who don't agree with them, as these takedowns are reminders of how wrong that person is because, theoretically, they need that reminder to be secure in their own identity. And thus, social categorization becomes so much more ingrained into the culture. We begin to see how social identity theory leads to prejudice, extremism, and even violence.[33]

Therefore, when you've seen how heavily the in-group that you're a part of hates all other out-groups, and how they treat those who are not in their in-group, it's not surprising if

---

38   Saul McLeod, "Social Identity Theory."

people feel a pressure (even unconsciously) to go along with the overarching thought process, too scared to disagree even slightly and risk losing their spot in the group.

The psychology of group thinking and our need to blend in to avoid humiliation is completely natural. When I was really young and my primary "in-group" was my family, I remember my sister and mom would frequently talk about how much they hated modern music, both preferring tunes from the '70s and '80s. I wasn't just embarrassed about my preference, but I felt wrong for having it. It felt like it was some secret I couldn't tell my family, or they would ridicule me. That's a tiny example of just how easy my brain can cause me to feel emotions that will pressure me to keep any opposing views I have with my in-group to myself.

But through this framework we lose the diversity of ideas and are stuck in the chokehold of either/or thinking.

Anytime anyone becomes concentrated, it means details and nuance and complexity is stripped away. A concentrated version of myself would be that I am a white, female, twenty-year-old student, which is true. I am. But I am so much more than that. And my relationship with age, race, gender, and school is slightly different than every other white, female, twenty-year-old student.

That is to say, something being concentrated leads to broad-brush simplification of the reality of that thing.

WHAT WILL HAPPEN TO US IN THE LONG RUN?

I interviewed Rabbi Elchanan Poupko, who had given a *TEDx Talk* on "The High Price of Political Polarization." Because of his position as a religious leader and clear interest in the topic, I wanted to hear his perspective on all of this.

He volunteers as a matchmaker in his community, and in doing this he realized to what extent things had changed. People were no longer interested in even meeting someone if they heard that person was of a different political leaning, something that was not the case a few years back.

"I've realized that it's becoming this either/or situation, no room for compromise or understanding," he said.

When I spoke to him about our obsession with the binary, I also asked if he had any tactics in viewing the world and its people as something made up by their real complexities.

"You can disagree with someone and engage in conversation that doesn't aim to change their opinions, but rather looks at their personhood. We jump to that because things become a lot more complex and difficult to understand when you empathize and acknowledge personhood," he said.

Rabbi Poupko talked to me about how we often paint people that we disagree with as "bad."

"People use it as a marketing tool because they know that painting things as black or white gets people angry and spurs them to take action. It perpetuates false radical thinking! Think about how the abortion argument is framed from both sides:

'are you pro-life, and the "others" believe in killing babies,' *or* 'are you a pro-choice, and the "others" hate women.'

"It works because, in the short term, that kind of argument is effective! It has a short-term benefit and a short-term result of people winning in an argument because they've painted it through this broad brush."

Yet ultimately, this pushes people to be more radicalized.

"Because it works in the short term," Rabbi Poupko said, "it pushes the people on the other side to reach your own levels of polarization, and all of a sudden you have people taking polar opposite views and seeing the other person as their enemy."

"It's short-term extremism, and it undermines any long-term ability to solve problems."

This sentence really struck me because it's what makes this whole ordeal so difficult. It's hard to change your thinking and your actions when you don't see how it affects you directly at the moment.

"The fights are fun; it feels good to win against someone you see as less than you," he said when answering my questions about whether people have an understanding of the dangers of polarization.

"But there is no success in that. Instead, we're making divisions our priority. We see that in politics, in our government, and in each other. We're enjoying these fights without looking outside to see how much it's weakening us."

The final thing Rabbi Poupko said is something I frequently think back to when I need to remember what this is all for.

"We are stuck here together, bound by our common humanity. We have to find the dignity of difference in the home that we all live in together."

And, when it comes to the reasoning for why we have to do this. I don't think there's a better explanation than that.

A MATTER OF SCHOLARS AND PHILOSOPHERS

My ideas of binary and broad-brushed thinking have grown and flourished because of my education in theories and philosophies. I read Michel Foucault's *Discipline and Punish* for class, and although I recognize that using arguments from old theories isn't always effective, I still think it was important to bring up this text, as it helped shape my broad thinking of how "us versus them" thinking is actually used as a tool by the systems of oppression to continue to grow toxic institutions.

In *Discipline and Punish,* Foucault explores the formation of a prison system, and he uses that example to point to similar structures in our everyday lives. How many institutions around us function in a way to ensure we are controlled and behave in the correct way for society?[39]

Foucault describes a prison called the "panopticon," structured to keep its prisoners in line by the idea that they are

---

39 Michel Foucault, *Discipline & Punish: The Birth of the Prison,* trans. Alan Sheridan.

being watched and monitored without ever being able to see anyone actually watching them. Foucault uses the example of the panopticon to explain how many of our other systems are set up in the same way. He argues many of the institutions around us are in ways systematic prisons, with the rules and expectations of society the invisible guards. This means there is no way for anyone to break from the systems and succeed in society, subjugating us all to the expectations of something other than our free will.

The system is so ingrained into society that you can't get rid of its issues by ridding the prison. It's a method of control that has spread, and now society itself is the systematic prison.

Foucault's whole point is how this system works because it's not some evil king decreeing punishment or some terrible overlords we need to dismantle to restore all the goodness back into society. It's institutions and systems that have spread that have entrenched control everywhere. And ultimately, what makes you unaware of that reality is the false binary narrative how we just need to topple something or defeat something to fix an issue that is what ultimately traps us.

Discipline and Punish showed me that the thing that keeps the prison running and functioning and growing is our lack of knowledge that it is all artificial. We buy into the false narrative, and we remain within the system, feeding into it and allowing it to quietly and secretly grow. Not change or better itself in growth but grow in the most literal sense: expand and enlarge, becoming an even greater, even more, inescapable prison for us.[34]

IT'S NOT A NARRATIVE. IT'S A SYSTEM.

As I said, when I was a kid, I loved reading. I especially loved fantasy books with kings and queens and evil tyrants and the "chosen one" heroes. I was one of the kids who stayed up late reading with flashlights, making up stories in my head of imaginary worlds and fantasies of me being the hero. I wanted to be called for a quest and be the main character of a story.

And there's nothing wrong with those books or a child's imagination. However, there is an issue that arises when we impose ideals of fictional narratives onto the reality of the world.

What Foucault's *Discipline and Punish* enlightened me on is that this desire to be the "good guy" against the "bad guy" was not just something that inspired me from multiple readings of *Harry Potter* or viewings of *Star Wars*. I was a product of my environment: a world that desperately wanted to categorize. As a society, we like to sort things into the neatest and clearest binary possible.[40]

We litter our world with labels and groupings that split people in half, regularly arguing "I am right" and "You are wrong." You can be this thing in this way or that thing in that way. We are us; they are them. What we must all come to realize, however, is that this binary is just a narrative ploy trying to get us to focus on the evil kings, the secret castles, the forbidden loves...rather than examining the real systems that create these narratives and critically examining who they benefit.

---

40   Ibid.

That's what it comes down to. It goes beyond just understanding *why* we like to paint things as black and white because that comes down to humans' desire for the millions of things we have to process every day to make sense. However, we do need to examine who it benefits when we allow ourselves to fall into binary thinking. Who gains power from citizens viewing their surroundings, each other, and themselves as holistically one thing or the other?

When you win in an argument with someone who you view as your opponent because of their opposing views, you may feel like you've had some sort of victory; like the progressives won the match today. But in fact, thinking this way simply reinforces systems that continue to oppress the beliefs and people we are trying to liberate.

Power comes from refusing to buy into the black and white narrative and demanding a new way of thinking because binary thinking holds us in place in some version of a prison. It traps us into thinking that there is a "bad" to defeat, and if we continue to exist in this society, the same way as we have always done, eventually we will find that source of evil and conquer it. But we never will.

WHY THE SOLUTION ISN'T "THINK ABOUT IT FROM THEIR PERSPECTIVE"

Just think about this whole notion of "you have to think about the other side." We've all heard these kinds of statements. That entire argument is structured under the binary idea that this is a two-sided system. The polarization and split in this country scare people, and they think the solution is just plain empathy and understanding the other side. But it's ultimately far more complex.

Think about what happens after a police officer murders a Black individual, especially if the Black person was armed or didn't immediately fall to their knees in front of the officer. People say, "Well, think about it from the police officer's perspective. What would you do if you were scared and you thought you were going to be attacked?"

But that excuse operates under the false notion that this is a binary two-sided issue and, thus, one side holds a solution. The issue does not stem from the one individual police officer or one individual Black person. The problem is that in a system that prioritizes punishment and violence and characterizes Blackness as something that is not only dangerous but less human, an institution like policing ultimately fails in its duty to protect and becomes yet another force that oppresses.

We sidestep the real problem when we focus our time finding who is to blame. It's true we should extend understanding and personhood to everyone; because the issue is never the individual, it is always the systems around us. But that doesn't mean the solution is just "putting yourself in their shoes for a minute." The solution is changing our mental frameworks to target the institutions and systems of power which operate in a way that allows these patterns to continue. If we ignore that, and spend time talking about "well, think about it from the 'other side'" or "we have to defeat the people who think that the officer was in the right," we inadvertently perpetuate the toxic system by ignoring its existence.

The solution is not to continue treating the other side like the enemy until they realize they've lost the war and now have to join our side. It's tackling the root of the issues and reimagining the systems that fail all of us.

EVERYTHING IS FAKE, AND THAT'S A GOOD THING!

It can be incredibly disheartening to detach from the idea of "valor and victory and heroes and villains," trading this mentality into a mindset of system acceptance; of realizing, acknowledging, and embracing that all this shit is completely artificial.

But it's actually in that admission that we can find hope. In this understanding we know we have the capacity to change. We have the capacity to view the world in a different way and not view one another as enemies because we acknowledge how that view is ultimately destructive.

Understanding that this idea is artificial grants us the most powerful weapon: choice. We can choose how we progress, how we think of things, and how we see one another, ourselves, and this country. And the answer is not choosing to all be infallible and good, pretending to exist on the correct side of a fictional binary. But choosing, instead, to grow; to push for change and progress as a collective.

Nothing in this world can be divided into a binary of choice. Change your mind.

CHAPTER 8

THE POLARIZED POLITICAL SYSTEM

———

Now that I just finished explaining mental frameworks of black and white thinking, I wanted to write a bit about two other colors that seem to put us all in a chokehold of simplified viewing of our country; the two colors that openly go to war every four years, or two years, or basically twenty-four seven around the clock, all the time…. I am, of course, talking about Red versus Blue, Right versus Left, elephant versus donkey, Republican versus Democrat—whatever you want to label this age-old country rivalry.

It's no coincidence that the word "polarization" is most associated with the word "political." There was actually a study that found Americans' strongest attachment was not to heritage or race or community, but actually to a political party. This seems insane when you consider the fact that millions of viable citizens don't actually vote. But when you begin to understand just how identity-based our politics have become, it may mean the political label has become a catch-all label on what kind of person you are.[41]

Because so many Americans consider political affiliation when judging the quality of someone's character, it's pretty clear we can't have a conversation around how a binary system leads to a polarized country without exploring politics.

MY LOVING REPUBLICAN PARENTS

When I was born, both my parents were republicans. Well, kind of. My dad was Canadian, so he was Republican in theory but not really in practice until 2009 when he became a citizen. My mother called herself a "fiscal conservative," meaning she still stood for liberal social issues but was interested in a reduced government. Then in 2004, the Iraq war flipped her vote. Since then, politics progressed in a way where she really couldn't prioritize her fiscal beliefs over the morality and behavior of the politicians representing the party. She's been a Democrat since 2004 and has never looked back.

My father, on the other hand, stuck to his "fiscal conservative" guns for much longer. Born in Canada, my dad's parents and family leans further to the right, mildly conservative by our American standards and wildly conservative by their Canadian ones. But he never had and never will have blind allegiance to a party. Maybe this is because he wasn't raised in this country, but I think he also had the privilege of getting a substantive education, which included a more critical evaluation on the reality of politics and politicians.

---

41   Milenko Martinovich, "Americans' Partisan Identities Are Stronger Than Race and Ethnicity, Stanford Scholar Finds."

Thus, even though he couldn't vote in 2008, he said he would have voted for Obama. He voted for Hillary Clinton in 2016, he voted for Stacey Abrams in the Georgia governor's race, he voted for Joe Biden in the 2020 general election, and he voted for Jon Ossoff and Raphael Warnock in the Georgia run-off. Because even if he is a fiscal conservative, he's a person first. He values decency, humanity, and leadership over party success.

I don't say this because I take pride in people knowing my parent's detailed voting history, nor because I'm trying to tell the story of how my parents left the dark side and joined the light. No, that's the opposite point I am trying to make.

The way we view our political opponents has changed, which is seen in the evidence. In 1960 a study found that 5 percent of Americans wouldn't like it if their kid married someone of a different political leaning. In 2010 that number jumped to 40 percent.[42] Think about that. Only a fifty-year difference and the number has skyrocketed.

When did we mix up and entrench identity into politics so much that we now view our political leanings as a label of the decency of our character?

My ideas around the US obsession with a black and white binary grew from watching our country cement as two opposing camps of enemies. The first president I remember being elected was Barack Obama. He came into office with the ring of liberal excitement, not just because of his skin

---

42   Jeremy Deaton, "In America, Politics Is the New Religion."

color, but because he stood for hope and change and was representative of a whole new liberal generation. Then the first president I voted against was Donald Trump, a man who normalized overt hateful speech and caused a modern peak of violence and hatred and fascism in the country.

So, why is it that we are so obsessed with categorizing all our thoughts and behaviors and standing into a black or white framework, or in this case, the red and blue one?

INCREASINGLY POLARIZED

Our politics have become increasingly polarized. From Ronald Reagan until today (save for maybe George H. W. Bush), there has not been a president that has not polarized the public and the parties, driving people further and further away from the semblance of general contentedness and increasingly in a scenario where one party is happy and the other is enraged.

Vox put out a chart in 2015 called "Our Increasingly Polarized Presidency, in One Chart." That chart reveals the average approval ratings among Republicans and Democrats for the president between 1951 and 2015. President Eisenhower, a Republican president who served from 1952 to 1961, had an average approval rating of 88 percent by Republicans and 49 percent by Democrats.[43] The idea of people from the opposing party today of the president giving them an almost 50 percent approval is so outrageous, I would be less surprised if someone told me they had been accepted to Hogwarts.

---

43   Andrew Prokop and Anand Katakam, "Our Increasingly Polarized Presidency, in One Chart."

And yes, it is true this is not the first time American politics has been extremely polarized. Take the Civil War, for example: a time where our polarization led to cries for secession and outright war. This historical event gives us a tangible example of just how far people will go if issues that separate a country aren't addressed.

In a study done by professors David W. Brady and Hahrie C. Han on political polarization, they used the Civil War era as a benchmark for total polarization. "The political parties then were not only widely separated ideologically but were highly unified around their respective positions, and the public seems to have been equally polarized."[44]

Today, our political identities have risen while the other things that might bind us together have fallen. Simon Kuper wrote, "Loneliness is contributing to our increasingly tribal politics," for the *Financial Times* where he points out that "fifty years ago, most people found identity through their family, church, neighborhood and (if male) their job and trade union. But these identities have steadily weakened. In short, many Americans and Britons lost their tribes. But now politics is creating new ones."[45]

This tribalism of our parties has just increased with the simultaneous growth of media coverage, something that leads to an easy echo chamber of the information and opinions you want to see.

---

44 Richard Walker, "Political Polarization—a Dispatch from the Scholarly Front Lines," *Issues in Governance Studies*, Special Edition (December 2006): 3.

45 Simon Kuper, "Loneliness is contributing to our increasingly tribal politics."

Today, we view polarization as a talking point, a statistic, or as grievance at a Thanksgiving dinner. But just how far does it have to go before it leads to violence or war? Turmoil, at its worst, leads to people cemented in their view, which leads to violence. And the fact is, we've become far more polarized. How can we let this continue to be the new normal given the reality of what that could mean?

HOW DID WE GET HERE?

To examine how we are in such a particular state of political polarization, we have to examine the phenomena of identity politics.

According to *Miriam-Webster*, it is "politics in which groups of people having a particular racial, religious, ethnic, social, or cultural identity tend to promote their own specific interests or concerns without regard to the interests or concerns of any larger political group.'"[46]

Despite this definition coming from a dictionary, I wanted to take a quick moment to acknowledge that the phrase "identity politics" was coined by the Combahee River Collective, a Black feminist lesbian organization founded in 1974 in Boston.[47]

Essentially, it means associating parts of your identity with your political preference. Although the rise of this as a widespread phenomenon is something that has occurred more recently, let's remember your identity was always important

---

46   *Merriam-Webster.com Dictionary*, s.v. "identity politics."

47   Arielle Gray, "This Boston Collective Laid the Groundwork for Intersectional Black Feminism."

if you were running to be a political figure. To get the far-
thest in status in politics (and in life), you had to look like
the American ideal.

If you couldn't check off all the following lists, people were
going to hesitate before casting a ballot.

Running for office and hoping not to cause any scandalous
headlines? Make sure you are all of the following:
☐ *White*
☐ *Male*
☐ *Straight*
☐ *Christian*
☐ *Loving father*
☐ *Devoted husband*

But when I talk about identity politics, I don't just mean how
the identity of our politicians factor into votes. I mean that
our own identities have started to bleed into our political
ones. And identity has been used more and more as a political tool by our elected officials.

Identity politics rose to popularity at the end of the twentieth
century with the rise of prominent social movements. These
groups and communities were no longer letting the reality of
their oppression be something that was silenced. The American ideal, the American dream, the American promise, all
things that politicians spout on and on about, is realistically
always out of reach for certain communities.

Therefore, it is not surprising that we saw the rise of new
Republican power through Ronald Reagan at an almost

simultaneous time as we saw these social movements enter the mainstream more and more—the idea of what it means to be an American and to reach success began to alter and fracture and change.

For people leaning to the left, it became a question of, "Okay, so you want me to vote you into power. What are you going to do about all these things happening to me or the communities I support?"

And on the right, it was, "Okay, so you want me to vote you into power. What are you going to do with these new movements and trends that are sullying what it means to be an American?"

POLARIZATION IS EASY

I spoke to Robert Charles Smith, a political scientist who is known for his work on politics and race, to get an expert's point of view on polarization and how we have reached such a breaking point in our government.

Smith has written and co-written books such as *Polarization and the Presidency: From FDR to Barack Obama, Contemporary Controversies and the American Racial Divide,* and *Conservatism and Racism and Why in America They Are the Same.*

I actually found him when watching a video on polarization, and he spoke about how politics is polarized because of the welfare versus taxes debate. I was watching that video and just thinking about how many Republicans and Democrats

I know who are my age, who if I asked them why they were Republicans or Democrats they absolutely would not talk about taxes, welfare, or government size, especially not the young Democrats I know. It's become so wrapped up in identity that at this point your political leanings are an outright symbol of what you believe regarding the way Americans live their lives, not the way that government functions and the tax legislation. I wanted to speak to Dr. Smith about this phenomenon.

When Dr. Smith first entered college, he wanted to be an American diplomat. Then the Vietnam War happened and changed everything. He knew he wanted to fight for civil rights, and his first career goal was going to be a lawyer and take that path to fight for Black liberation. After a meeting with his academic advisor about his wishes, he was informed that he could actually do more for the Black liberation movement as a scholar.

In response to my queries on his specific interest in polarization, he informed me that for the book *Polarization and the Presidency: From FDR to Barack Obama,* he initially just wanted to focus on the polarization that occurred as a result of the election of President Obama.

"We knew that Obama was going to be polarizing—racially, politically, and ideologically polarizing," he admitted. But when he and his co-author began to research the origins of polarizing, they began to see a pattern of polarization (or lack thereof) caused by the presidency starting with Franklin Roosevelt.

I asked Dr. Smith, "I know you've spoken on how gridlock comes from this debate between welfare and taxes. However, in recent years, how much of our political gridlock derives from identity politics? And does this lead us to be incapable of separating the person from their political beliefs and separate political beliefs from personhood?"

"Well, I think there is no doubt that identity politics occurs more and more," he said. "Racial identity is very polarizing."

And as much as racial identity is a human right and we might wish our politics existed separately from that, race has been a part of our political discussion since the foundations of this country. Our country views capital as its number one goal, and a great deal of this country's early acquisitions of capital was on the backs of Black slaves who were seen as the property of their rich owners. In other words, they were their capital as well as their tools for capital.

So, as much as we want to say that identity isn't political or to create a narrative that identity politics is unique to today, it's impossible to erase the reality of our country's history. However, the overt nature of identity in our politics, the way it has been used as a tool for politicians to wield, isn't what we've seen consistently through history and is something very prevalent today.

"What's interesting about racial identity being so openly talked about in our modern politics, and used as a political tactic, is that it's fairly new. Obama and Clinton tip-toed around race, whereas Trump uses it as part of his politics," Dr. Smith said. "And as facets of our personal identity such as race, feminism, and sexuality become increasingly unabashedly political, political polarization is now spilling into the personal."

WE REALLY DON'T LIKE EACH OTHER!

And there's no denying the truth of this. In their article, "What Is the True Cost of Polarization in America?" Zaid Jilani and Jeremy Adam Smith talk about fourteen negative outcomes of polarization in our country. They covered studies that examined topics from family relationships to the change in our geographical makeup.

We've all heard the phenomena of "the racist family members," and more and more people dreading time spent with extended family. But this isn't just a saying. It's actually been proven that Thanksgiving dinners with families made up of folks in different parties are actually shorter than they were before. "The researchers estimated that thirty-four million person-hours of cross-partisan discourse were eliminated in 2016 thanks to this polarization effect."[48]

Polarization isn't just happening in our ideologies; it's also showing itself where people decide to live. This "self-segregation of Americans into like-minded communities" was named "the Big Sort" by Bill Bishop in 2004. A study done by Ron Johnston, David Manley, and Kelvyn Jones in *Annals of American Association of Geographers* examined three spatial scales: the fifty states, nine broad census regions, and

---

48 Zaid Jilani and Jeremy Adam Smith, "What Is the True Cost of Polarization in America?"

over three thousand counties. They found that "over the two decades and six elections between 1992 and 2012 there has been greater spatial polarization in the percentage voting for the Democratic Party candidates in presidential elections."[49]

In addition, according to research done by Pew Research Center, 49 percent of Republicans say the Democratic party makes them feel afraid, while 55 percent of Democrats say the same thing about the Republican Party.[50]

Meanwhile, 52 percent of Republicans say Democrats are more close-minded than other Americans, and 70 percent of Democrats say Republicans are the close-minded ones.[45]

Over 50 percent of individuals who identify as Republican or Democrat do so because of a view that the other party as bad for the country. Meaning, 50 percent of people's political ideologies is built on reactionary fear.[45]

I cite these statistics because I need to be clear that political polarization is not just a saying that people use. It's not a theory. It's happening in practice, affecting our institutions and the folks in them.

A common argument I've seen progressives make is that people use the rhetoric of "we don't want to be polarized" as an excuse to be too "centrist" in their ideals; that people use the fight against polarization as an excuse to not lean all the way to the left, where many progressives argue you should be if you have any decency or morals.

---

49 Richard Florida, "America's 'Big Sort' Is Only Getting Bigger."
50 "Partisanship and Political Animosity in 2016."

The conversation around polarization is avoided or ignored because "If my opinion is polarizing, so what? It's what needs to be said. Fuck everyone who thinks the opposite. They're monsters." Yet, the truth of the matter is that polarization is dangerous, and we can't ignore the consequences, no matter how righteous we believe our opinions are.

VIOLENCE IS NEVER THE ANSWER, UNLESS THE QUESTION IS WHAT HAPPENS WHEN WE'RE POLARIZED.

Dr. Smith spoke to me about the worst possible outcome of polarization, and he was quite blunt. "The worst outcome would be violence. The way polarization normally ends in politics is one party indecisively wins. Right now, we're undoubtedly going toward a Democratic majority, which could lead to the right being violent."

And the problem is this result of violence when things don't go the way that one group wants it to seems more and more like a possibility.

Forty-five percent of Republicans now view Democratic policies as a threat, up from 37 percent in 2014. And 41 percent of Democrats say the same about the Republican Party's policies, an increase of 10 percentage points from two years ago.[51]

The rhetoric of threat becoming more and more popular is showing us how this increase in polarization is moving us to a place of violence.

---

51   Ibid.

We've seen hate crimes and violence quite often in recent years spurred by issues of identity: religion, race, culture, and sexuality. "Hate crimes in the US rose by 17 percent in 2017, the third straight year that incidents of bias-motivated attacks have grown, according to the FBI."[52] And this is certainly influenced by the rise of polarization.

In an article, "What Is the True Cost of Polarization in America?" Jilani and Smith point to a 2018 study that shows increasing indications of 'partisan identity strength' meaning, there your label of Democrat or Republican is becoming more and more a part of your identity.[53]

The article by Jilani and Smith quote Lilliana Mason, a political scientist: "It makes sense that as an identity grows stronger, and conflict intensifies, people will begin to approve of violence."[48]

When our in-groups become more and more defined, we begin to see the out-groups increasingly in a negative light. As we become more isolated, we begin to see them more as the opposing side, as the side that is fundamentally in the wrong, and, in that mindset, we begin to see violence as a justifiable response to these wrongdoers.

I interviewed Dr. Smith in July of 2020 and revised and worked on this book's draft on January 27, 2021, exactly three weeks after the insurrection at the capitol. I remember when Dr. Smith told me how the worst outcome would be violence,

52 "FBI: Spike in US hate crimes for third year in a row."
53 Zaid Jilani and Jeremy Adam Smith, "What Is the True Cost of Polarization in America?"

and I was startled. For me, the idea of terror and weapons and murders happening because of political affiliations was the topic of my history or fantasy books. I never thought about it for my current reality. And yet, after he explained, it made sense. When we are pulled further and further into our opposing sides and people are increasingly radicalized to view the other as the enemy, resorting to violence makes sense.

Just like on January 6, I was horrified; I was disgusted; I was mad. But I, just like many others, wasn't surprised.

The actions that happened on that day have just continued to show me just how necessary it is for us to take a radical stance in pushing for change. Because our current world and our current mental frameworks have allowed us to reach a point where I can see people shattering windows to break into the US Capitol to inflict violence and overturn our democracy. And I'm not surprised.

THE TWO-PARTY SYSTEM

The polarization has led us to question our trust in core institutions.

But the thing is, a two-party system is not the root of our issues. I thought it was when I first started exploring this problem. I was convinced that the most toxic institution of our nation was the two-party system, holding us in a chokehold of the binary.

However, speaking to Dr. Smith altered my view on this: "A two-party system is not in and of itself polarizing, but it can become one, in a polarized environment," he said. "When we are in a polarized environment, it reinforces polarization, and polarization reinforces it. But it is not one creating the other."

And that's the thing. Once again, the answer is not simple. There's not one thing we can point to and blame, change, and fix all our polarization.

The polarization of politics using identity as a tool to turn people against one another is beneficial to politicians in the short term with the price of long-term ineffectiveness. But despite that, politicians use it because they need immediate victories.

Let's take the pro-life versus pro-choice argument, for example. What a woman does with her body and her pregnancy doesn't exactly sound like a conversation that would spark around the size of our government now. Does it? No, but we still see every single senator and congressperson stand up and declare their opinions on the matter. And the matter gets so much news coverage. Pundits talk about it, Twitter activists talk about it, hell, I think it's one of the first things I learned about that should be a reason "you don't want to be Republican." If I want to talk about my body and reproduction, there is no escaping the political lens that it now lives through.

Even though the pro-life versus pro-choice argument isn't actually what most politicians spend their days creating legislation, they still are far more public about this issue than they are about their stand on a new bill that will build more highways, hypothetically. This is because showing they're either pro-choice or pro-life helps cement their base. Democrats want to hear that the people representing them are strongly and loudly pro-choice. Many Republican voters want to hear from their politicians that they value religion and Christian values, thus, they stand against abortion. For many people (especially primary voters, who tend to be the more engaged voters and more polarized people), it's a big factor in whether someone will get your vote or not.

I write this just weeks after the death of Justice Ginsberg. The actions that followed stand as hard evidence of our identity politics bleeding into politics. The justice's replacement immediately circulated fear for the power of the supreme court in rulings regarding voter suppression, reproductive rights, and rights of marriage, as just a few examples. The change in conversation to focus on justices and how they relate to rulings on things that make up our identity is very likely going to be a tipping point in the election. It took mere moments to go from mourning to political action.

The death of Justice Ginsberg is a quintessential example of how politics becoming a part of our identity has, in some ways, helped in the movement. Because more than ever people are engaged and involved. But at what cost? As it gets more polarized and the political bleeds into everyone's personal, the political has become more entrenched in our identities while all humanity has been sucked out of politics.

The night of her death, Democrats raised millions of dollars for races across the country, and days after her death the GOP was united in confirming a new justice.

The fact of the matter is that identity politics is now just a tool in a politician's toolbox. Democrats are not intrinsically better people than Republicans. They just know that their base is more encouraged if they make speeches supporting more progressive thought—because we are polarized.

In a polarized country, when you have two sides like this, you're always going to see the side you're on as the "good guys" and the other side as the "bad guys."

A polarized environment, and subsequently a polarized politics, draws a harsh line in the sand between who is on side A and who is on side B. It makes the binary so distinct and all-encompassing of our society.

Our politics aren't moving. We've taken gridlock as an excuse for the government not to work because it feeds into our binary mindset. Polarization is so easy, it's so attractive, and it's not surprising. It's a feedback loop. When we become more polarized, we have more reason to be polarized.

A thing we hear all the time is: "I'm not going to compromise on human rights." And we absolutely shouldn't. Racism, homophobia, sexism, and classism are all things that are not a political argument. So, why are they so interwoven into our politics? Because it keeps people apart. It drives people against one another and into their base.

We win the battle, but we're all losing the war.

WHAT CAN WE DO?

Honestly, polarization is an epidemic. It's completely ingrained in us at this point, and it feeds from one system to the other: Enforcing polarization, pushing people more into their beliefs, more polarization occurs, polarization is used as a tool, we become more polarized, we enforce more polarization.

I referenced Foucault and the theory of the panopticon in a previous chapter. The panopticon was a jail that functioned because of the invisible nature of the guards. You are imprisoned in walls where you cannot see your guards or who is surveilling you. The proper behavior is not enforced by real figures. Prisoners will police themselves when they believe they are under constant surveillance.

Polarization is like Foucault's panopticon: the invisible system that spreads throughout the prison without us noticing how we are taking part in the system that is slowly hurting us.

We have to change our frameworks from blaming one another and seeing each other as opposition to look at what systems have created oppositional forces as the driving force of our government and what can we do to change this.

Nobody is the enemy, and we do not prevail if we "defeat" the other side. We prevail if we change our frameworks to "I empathize with you and I am willing to work for a better country for both you and me." We make real sustainable progress when we look at the big picture, seeing that the problem doesn't come from "these people who have to be rooted out because they are problematic" and rather from zooming out and realizing that we have to change the way the system works so it doesn't create people who can't see the difference between political ideology and a human right.

It's so difficult because oftentimes the people who we are so polarized against are degrading or ignorant or offensive or even violent. And the way to fix the system is obviously not to engage with people who are radicalized to hate you, but to understand and acknowledge, in your mind, that it is not "natural" someone is like that. In fact, it's because of our unnatural toxic systems that prop themselves to look normal and natural that enforce polarization and lead to this kind of thinking.

I take the time and try to remind myself that I don't hate anybody of the opposing party. I hate what has become of our political systems that use identity and social groupings to polarize the public and win elections.

We advance through empathy, listening, and understanding, rethinking how we view one another and rethinking what we will accept as our politics.

To work for something that is revolutionary we have to choose this radical empathy and redistribution of energy from a group of people to an overall system. The empathy that is chosen here is incredibly difficult. And when I say empathy, I don't mean listening or engaging with the views of people who choose violence or ignore the humanity of certain groups. I mean acknowledging that these people have fallen victim to systems in this country that are set up to drive people to these radical places. Empathizing means understanding that and making the incredible choice not to hate the individual as your form of advocacy but instead channel that anger toward the systems that create these kinds of toxic mindsets.

I choose to build mindsets toward the "other side" that say "even if you think you hate me, I don't hate you. I hate the systems that have allowed your thinking and hatred of me to be normalized, and that's what I will seek to change. And I will work to make a better country, one that's better for all of us, whether you are with me or not."

We are not seeking progress for the victory of "our side." Change your mind.

PART III

CHANGING
THE WORLD

CHAPTER 9

WHY IT'S POSSIBLE

"But is any of this even possible?"

That was something I asked myself quite a bit when I first started thinking about this concept of mental frameworks as a key component of progressive change. You can't expect people to just stop having mindsets that simplify things, as these frameworks are often instinctual. And you can't really *force* someone to make the effort to change their mind.

But I've realized (and a lot of this realization actually happened over the course of my experience writing this book) just how much of a difference is made by being aware of how my mind operates in these limiting ways and by making the choice to change that mindset. And I've realized just how possible it is to change my view of the world when I begin to realize change is needed.

The thing is, I wrote this book not only because I noticed these subject matters weren't being addressed by those who were seeking real change but because I noticed within myself that I had some pretty messed up thinking about the world.

I was spiteful and angry and blaming everything around me for the issues we have. I was blaming things that did legitimate harm, and yet it didn't bring me any closer to hope for tomorrow when I spent every waking moment seeking things to be mad about for today. And even in the process of writing this book, I have noticed a real change in my thinking. I'll catch myself about to say generalized statements of hatred and think, *You know, I really probably shouldn't do that.*

I'm more willing to hear people out. I get less personally invested in every debate or argument I have. I work to remind myself to hate systems that have oppressed communities and turned us against one another rather than hating individuals.

And I'm certainly nowhere near the point in my life where the instinct is to view things as gray rather than black or white. But every day I remind myself of the importance of accepting people as complicated, and how I need to strive for progress as a whole not factions. By doing this work, it feels like I'm taking a genuine step toward becoming a person who wants the future to look better.

Mindset is only one small part of progress. It's only one piece of the puzzle of a future that is sustainable for the many, not the few.

But addressing the issue of how to change our minds means embracing the human factor of change. The world changes when we push it to change.

THE POWER OF BELIEF

Cynicism is the enemy. It's not a person or a group or a political affiliation. It's a disbelief that we can't achieve better.

The truth is we can all be better. We can all do more, we can all reassess our internal biases.

The idea that if you "believe it then you can achieve it" is, I'll admit, a corny phrase. But I have to believe that's true. Because what the hell is the alternative? It's lack of hope for the future, lack of hope in ourselves, and lack of hope in those around us that stops us from achieving greatness.

The only way we create a better tomorrow is if we believe that it's a possibility, and if we believe that, we are a genuine part of that creation.

Understand that the world we live in and the people we are don't exist in separate vacuums. We interact with one another: the world creates us, and we create the world. Because of that, the work to change our minds and make it a place that is more open to complicated stories and nuanced people and human success and error will help create that better tomorrow.

I watched a *TED Talk* by Pascale Murphy, a professor who gave a talk called, "Moving Beyond Cynicism: Creating the World We Want to See."

He spoke about this experience he had when he put a pride flag outside his house. The flag was stolen, which at first did not deter Murphy. He quickly replaced the flag, only for it to be stolen once again. In response, Murphy added two more flags at a place slightly more out of reach. Then, someone spray-painted anti-gay rhetoric on his sidewalk and slashed his tires.

Murphy explains despite how he was energized to fight back at the beginning, as this continued, he was starting to get angry and suspicious and worried about all of those around them. And that's when the cynical view started to settle in. Murphy says, "I started to hate back.... This, my friends, is the breeding ground for cynicism. A cynicism that is sustained by the distrust of those around us and the complete disengagement with that which is meaningful in life."

He started to feel hopeless and dejected, "What use is it to take positive actions if you're just going to be hated for it," Murphy says. This feeling remained until he got a letter from a fellow neighbor about inclusivity that had been sent to the neighborhood. Murphy went to go visit that neighbor to talk about his experience. As a result, Murphy and his neighbors decided to have a barbecue and create the organization "Neighbors for Inclusion." This barbecue brought friends in with lots of media and volunteers coming and offering places to have events. People just showed up and showed out in solidarity to this issue.

It was a massive thing. Murphy now saw pride flags up and down the street in his neighborhood. He was getting the attention of the media and getting positive feedback from complete strangers. He tells a touching story of a five-year-old who rang the doorbell and said, "I love rainbows!" before presenting the cake she had made for the barbecue, a cake with wobbly icing saying "Love + Peace."

"If this story ended with me walking out the front door and hating the world, none of this would have happened," Murphy says. "And this was tempting, very tempting.... But I decided to work for the world that I wanted."

Murphy's story encapsulates so much of the meaning behind what I'm trying to say: the power of working for the world we want to see and believe in the possibility of something better. Another thing in Murphy's story that struck me was how easily cynicism can isolate you from the possibility of humanity.

By deciding to have the barbeque and start this small organization for him and his neighbors, he got the attention of hundreds, if not thousands. He gained hope and a new sight of the people around him. Rather than perpetuating a never-ending cycle of hatred and actions against one another, he did something else. And you know what? It turns out there were far more people in his community interested in going to a barbecue for inclusivity than taking down a pride flag in a man's front yard.

If Murphy was the cynic, he would view the world as the place where we put up a pride flag, the flag is stolen, and no matter how many times we put it back up, it's stolen again. What's the point in fighting for a world like that? Murphy didn't act in a reactionary way that would lead to spiteful vengeance. Instead, he took actions to do something good. It wasn't retaliation; it was an action that was for a different way of thinking and invited the communities around him to join him in his new way of thinking.

There is such power in hope and belief because that is the root of change. As Murphy said in the talk, "Change happens when we refuse to simply reflect the world we are presented with and instead reflect the world we wish to see."[54]

THE POWER OF THE PEOPLE

I recently swiped through a dating app and matched with this guy. It was the same old boring conversation, neither of us very committed to constant engagement (nothing like a global pandemic to really take the pizzazz out of online dating apps), but he asked me where I worked.

I told him where I was interning, which was at End Citizens United as their digital/communications intern and on the Rock the Vote fall intern team. When he heard about End Citizens United and I explained in more detail about the work the organization does to try to root big and corrupt money out of politics, he said, "Oh, that must get depressing to see all that bad shit on a day-to-day basis."

And genuinely, until that moment, I had never considered how the work I was doing was considered depressing. And then I started to think about why, in my time getting more and more engaged, deeper into the political world, more exposed to just how impossible it is to have even the

---

54   *TEDx Talks*, "Moving Beyond Cynicism: Creating the World We Want to See | Pascal Murphy | TEDxRyersonU."

smallest dent on the biggest issues, I had somehow become more hopeful.

But the answer is obvious. I knew the moment I took two seconds to think about it: It's the people.

Working in these environments exposes me to great people. They're hardworking, dedicated, creative, open-minded, and dreamers. They are the most patriotic people, who work to strive for the more perfect union that is promised in our country's foundational documents, as far as I'm concerned. And it's inspiring to see what they can do and what journey brought them here.

We always hear about all the bad stuff going on in the world. We always know when the government fucked up and something has happened that makes us all groan and say, "This cannot possibly be our country. This cannot be the leader of the free world and the land of opportunity." But what we don't get on the news is the massive coalition of people who are fighting, every day, to right these wrongs.

And, then of course, I am inspired when seeing the sheer amount of people who are waking up to the need for change. Between May and August of 2020, the Armed Conflict Location and Event Data Project (ACLED) reports there have been over 10,600 demonstrations and protests across the country for racial justice.[55]

---

55 "Demonstrations and Political Violence in American: New Data for Summer 2020."

In 2018 Gen Z and millennials proved their political engagement by outvoting older generations in the 2018 midterms, according to PEW research. "The three younger generations—those ages eighteen to fifty-three in 2018—reported casting 62.2 million votes, compared with 60.1 million cast by baby boomers and older generations."[56]

There's the constant inspiration from observing people my age being actively conscious of issues in the world and taking real action. There are incredible organizations like the Sunrise Movement, an organization self-titled as the "army of young people." Their goal is to elect government officials who will actively work to combat climate change. Or there's GoodKids MadCity, which was established by high school students in the wake of the Parkland school shooting. Now, the organization works to combat the roots of problems for people in low-income areas, such as access to mental health, steady employment, and after-school programs. And that's just naming two of literally hundreds of organizations and movements and work that younger people are doing each day about fixing the problems they see.[57]

Just in my two years of exposure to these people and my twenty years in this generation all lead up to this breaking point. I know that the possibility for real change exists because there is real want in a very large number of people to make the country better. That's why I wrote this book

---

56 Anthony Cilluffo and Richard Fry, "Gen Z, Millennials and Gen X Outvoted Older Generations in 2018 Midterms."

57 Sophia Tulp, "5 Nonprofits That Are Changing the World—All Led by Young People."

because I know there are so many people out there looking to do anything and everything in our quest for progress.

THE INFINITE POSSIBILITY OF THE HUMAN'S MIND

We all know that we have the drive and the determination to make this country a better place. The people are there, and we have the capacity to add to our movement and change mental frameworks to help better the movement by bettering ourselves each and every day.

The human mind does the extraordinary. It can strategize for power, it can remember stories and histories, it can be compassionate, it can be hateful, and it thinks of better tomorrows.

Our minds dictate how we view the world, and how we view the world dictates if we believe we can change it. Adjusting and changing our mental frameworks must be considered one of the factors of this country's current revolution.

We are humans with an incredible capacity for change, and we are in a moment created by people with the real itch to do something about everything we see that isn't right. And that's why I know this is possible. I believe in the possibility of humans and the potential of humankind.

CONCLUSION

———

When I was describing my book to one of my interviewees, they described it as the "manifesto of a young person living in today's time who sees issues and wants to do something about them." Which...kind of, yes.

2020, HISTORY, AND ME

We are at a tipping point in history. I mean, how many conversations have you had this year that had the words "these unprecedented times...?" What were you doing while the world unraveled and tried to right itself? Nothing like being forced to break out of everyone's regular routine to realize that maybe those habits shouldn't be natural.

The year 2020: the pandemic, the protests, the election. Enough content to fill a full-length fictional series of novels, if only you could get the concept of the story past an editor because, chances are, they would tell you the story wouldn't be believable enough.

So here we are, after the most bizarre and busy and depressing and uplifting and horrifying year, it feels like, at this point, we've all been on edge for months. The idea of what is normal has been thrown out the window, both by context and by choice.

The world is changing, that is certain. But the way we change it evolves. That's where we are able to come in and seize the control we've lost on such a massive scale this year.

I wrote this book not because I'm an expert, not because I have faced any particular hardship that others haven't, and not because I think any of the work that people have done in spaces of advocacy and progress should be discredited or ignored. I am literally just a twenty-year-old girl who had a thought—a thought that I didn't think enough people were considering, and I wanted to make at least a few people think about what I had to say; just consider my view and bring it into the picture of what we define as "work to change the world."

We get too caught up in reacting to everything bad. We're so busy thinking of ways to fight back, to paint ourselves as heroes and others as villains, that we don't think about the new thing we're trying to build.

It's mental framework versus reactionary thinking. It's changing how we view the world and each other as the catapult to tangible holistic change versus reacting to the things that displease us, ultimately reinforcing its existence by constantly reaffirming the systematic issues in our idea that we need to react, retaliate, and defeat a problem that is ingrained within all of us.

We need to recognize that changing ourselves and changing our minds is key to the change we want to create. Forgetting that or ignoring it could lead to a twisted version of what we have today: better on the surface, but equal systems of oppressions rooting us in place, never allowing true growth.

MAKE IT COMPLICATED

Everything I talked about in this book boils down to one idea: Make it complicated.

It's one of the core themes that come up in the sections of this book—the need for nuance and the ultimate power that comes from accepting the complex human.

We have to acknowledge that our past is made up of complicated humans and a different context than what we live in today. In our country's history, there are things we absolutely should be ashamed of and acknowledge as causing irreversible harm. However, if we exist with frameworks of erasing the parts of our history and strictly ignoring or demonizing the things that were bad, we lose the ability to grow from the past. We lose the ability to think critically of what made us who we are today. What happened before has caused who we are now.

Another thing I talk about in detail is the tendency to categorize and form in-groups and out-groups within our geographical locations—something that can seem like a small and ultimately unimportant thing, but can, in the end, cause a lot of damage. This notion that we should divide, or we should separate each other and stereotype one another, harms an ultimate movement for progress. We don't get there by finding a thing to blame, like a geographical location or a person who comes from a certain area of the country. That is yet another example of our instincts to simplify and boil a person down to one thing so we know if we want to accept or reject them. But ultimately, changing our frameworks to view things around us as nuanced and complicated moves us to a place where we're ready to change our toxic systems of power rather than defeat the people or places that are a symptom of the issue.

Finally, in this book I wrote about our binary thinking and polarization. How polarized we are today, where that came from, why it's like this…all that polarization is justified. I am not demonizing those who view people in this country as "the other side" and think there's a group of people in this country "who need to be defeated." The hardest part about polarization is that the media and those in power justify those feelings. But the reality is to achieve real progress, we need to change our frameworks from this view. Polarization constantly makes us operate in reactionary thoughts and actions; it doesn't allow for collective growth. As easy as it is to become polarized, it's imperative we fight the mindsets that try to put us in opposing groups. Polarization strengthens harmful binary thinking that people, places, moments, and history exist in a black or a white space. But ultimately, everything is in the gray. We have to work to change our minds to think of the world in the gray, not in the made-up absolutes of black and white that are painted all around us.

All these things ultimately come down to seeing ourselves and each other as intricate people. People aren't inherently good or bad. No one is evil and no one is a blessed hero. Every single person gets up every morning and goes through a day and goes to bed at night. And throughout that day, we all live completely different lives.

Hundreds of millions of different lives are being lived in this country. Billions of lives are being lived in this world. And every single one of those people see the world in a different way. Every single person experiences the world in a different way. No one is the same, and no one is experiencing the same world. That reality is one of the most wonderful things about humanity.

My point in emphasizing this is that we do not acknowledge the humanity that each person has. Every person has a reason for their thoughts and their opinions, whether it's because they have a need for power and authority at any cost necessary, or they're a person who needs to fight for climate change. Both of those people have a reason for what made them who they are. They both have a reason and a life and a purpose that led them to their goals.

Each person's position in life and society led them to the mental frameworks they have.

But we know our mental frameworks can change. We know we can change our minds. And I hope I've shown you why the work is valuable for the efforts of sustainable progress.

WRITING A BOOK

The experience I've had writing this book has been quite turbulent. It's difficult to write a book addressing "our current time" when truly every day is a new headline, a new story, and a new moment.

When I first started writing I was obsessed with the concept of being "tomorrow's history." It came with this fascination that I had about how we are living in such a huge moment in history. But the idea of the book came in the wake of the pandemic. In the months that followed, a lot more happened. History was occurring every day with every new headline and every new "breaking news" moment.

I realized it was a waste of time to be consumed by the idea of "tomorrow's history" and how that specifically will be affected by the moment we're in. It doesn't matter if there's a massive civil rights movement, a historic election, or a global pandemic. We are always creating the next generation's history.

And that awakening spurred the rest. I started to think about what it was that truly creates history. It's not a moment—it's the people; the people who interact with the time and the place they're in, whether that's deciding to go to the grocery store one day or deciding to start an organization to combat climate change in your local neighborhood.

Tomorrow will be affected by everything we do today. It doesn't matter who we are or what we do. Our mark will be left on the future. We impact the world in everything we do, and we all contribute to the history that the next generation will learn.

So, I let go of the original concept and started focusing on the idea that, at the core of everything humans are, what matters is not the grandiose idea of a "lasting legacy for history." From that grew the idea that humans are complicated, and the world is complicated, so why does so much in my mind want to fight against that reality?

In the process, I've spoken to incredible people: people who have dedicated their lives to education and to advocacy; people who have lived through over three times the amount of history that I've experienced; people who have truly seen the horrible in the best of times and wonderful in the worst of times.

I've gotten to research and think constantly about the generation I'm part of and this moment that we're living in. I've researched people who've been talking about the things I just realized for their whole lives. In my internships, all advocacy groups focused on the world of politics, and for the past few months I've been jotting down quotes and ideas from when a fellow intern or coworker or superior says something that I found pertinent. Getting to live in the world from the perspective of "I believe we can change. How can I convince others?" was something I thought was going to be difficult or unenjoyable. Quite to my shock, it turned out to be an incredibly eye-opening experience.

I wrote a book about understanding and appreciating nuance in each other and the world around us. I wrote it because I believe it to be an important issue, and not because I'm the CEO of this mental framework thinking. I know we view things in black and white and are drawn to simple answers, not just because I've seen people do it or because of the research I've done. It's because I did it. I *still* do it! I have so often viewed things in a way that wasn't effective.

So, I wrote this book to change my own mind, as well as others.

And although it's a continuous and constant effort, although it's never my instinct, it's never what's easy, and it never seems quite fair, it's improved how I view things and understand the world.

CHANGE YOUR MIND, CHANGE THE WORLD

I was watching a YouTube video from a woman named Natalie Wynn under the username "ContraPoints." Wynn makes these incredible video essays breaking down arguments and theories on politics, gender, ethics, race, and philosophy. Each insightful video is done with as many wigs, sets, and costumes that one could ever wish for.

In one of her videos titled "The Left," there's an argument between two characters, both played by Wynn. The first character is an extreme leftist who stands for destruction and radical revolution to overthrow the government. The other character argues about the true effectiveness of that radical stance and how to best create change when the game is rigged against us and the issues are deep-rooted in all of us and the systems we interact with every day.[58]

And at the end of the video, one of the concluding arguments is this:

---

58   *ContraPoints,* "The Left | ContraPoints," September 24, 2017, video, 14:01.

"You can't just win the war in the street; you also have to win the war in the heart and the mind."

And doesn't that just boil my point down beautifully to one sentence?

As I think about future generations, we still have an opportunity to make sure their future looks better than ours. That they are living in a world that doesn't operate in absolutes, that has fought systems that oppress people, that silences communities, that ensures certain demographics or groups are the only ones who get to rise through the ranks.

And that world starts today. It starts with us changing the way we think of ourselves, each other, and our country.

A person can change. Our minds can change. Our mental frameworks can be changed. We have to believe that because nobody is evil, and nobody is good. We're all just vessels with brains who have neurons that fire to make us have thoughts that turn into action. Anybody and everybody can change. And anybody and everybody should want to change.

Change your mind from the idea that you're right, and people who disagree with you are wrong.

Change your mind from the idea that we have to place blame on individuals for our current issues and our past ones.

Change your mind from the thought that there are people who are naturally evil.

Change your mind from concepts that dwindle down anyone's humanity.

Change your mind to make empathy something you always work for first and words and action something you decide to do second.

Change your mind that you can't make a difference just from changing your mind.

Change your mind from the idea that you can't change the world.

You have this incredible thing called your mind. A malleable thing with neurons that fire that create the ever-changing person that you are.

You're a complicated, interesting, imperfect human being.

What can't you do?

ACKNOWLEDGEMENTS

———

First off, I'd like to thank everyone who read this book. I know I'm writing about something really complex, and I know I'm not any kind of expert or genius on the subject. I'm just a person who had an idea, so I want to thank everyone who was willing to open their minds to what I had to say.

I also want to thank my family. Thank you to my dad, for accepting that his daughter is a liberal (I know that's hard for you); to Gabrielle, for always bullying me; and to my mom, for reading my drafts, being my editor, and the person I most look up to.

I want to thank all my friends, in particular: Grant Bishko and Travis Harper. To Grant, thank you for dealing with me in the stage of this book when I was just mind dumping all my thoughts, staying up until 4 a.m. in your dining room to type fifteen thousand words that I inevitably had to delete or rewrite. To Travis, thank you for always listening and engaging in the most thought-provoking conversations with me. Half the content in this book is inspired from our talks, and I know this book wouldn't exist without the influence you've had on my life.

To everyone at New Degree Press, particularly Whitney Jones and Faiqa Zafar, thank you for helping me turn a few wild ideas written on a piece of paper into a book.

Finally, to everyone else who I haven't directly mentioned yet, who contributed to my early fund and supported my book before I had even finished, you're amazing and I love you all. I wish I could write you all personalized notes that I could publish in this book, but alas, we will have to live with just a named acknowledgment.

In alphabetical order, thank you to:

Amy Schuman, Ana Maria Storino, Anthony Lupu, Austin Hand, Ava Straccia, Cailyn Carr, David Bishko, Dom Letterii, Joan G. de Pontet, Elizabeth McGraw, Eric Koester, Erin Wilson, Grace Schepis, Julia Glade Bender, Kate Rodgers, Kathryn Smith, Koby Polaski, Natalie Gambardella, Nicholas Goudie, Stella Storino, Pablo Patel, Pascale Baillargeon, Rachel Wood, Veronique Laniel, Vivianne Ivanier, and Yan Tougas.

APPENDIX

INTRODUCTION

Brenan, Megan. "Americans' Trust in Mass Media Edges Down to 41 Percent." Gallup, September 26, 2019. Accessed January 22, 2021. https://news.gallup.com/poll/267047/americans-trust-mass-media-edges-down.aspx.

Mapping Police Violence. "Police Violence Map." Accessed July 15, 2020. https://mappingpoliceviolence.org/.

Rainie, Lee, Scott Keeter, and Andrew Perrin. "Americans' Trust in Government, Each Other, Leaders." Pew Research Center—US Politics and Policy, September 18, 2020. https://www.pewresearch.org/politics/2019/07/22/trust-and-distrust-in-america/.

CHAPTER 1

Christian, Brian and Tom Griffiths. *Algorithms to Live By: The Computer Science of Human Decisions.* New York: Henry Holt and Co., 2016.

Cloer, Dan. "Rethinking Our Mental Framework." Vision.org, 2004. Accessed January 22, 2021. https://www.vision.org/ rethinking-our-mental-framework-677.

Dictionary.com, s.v. "Positionality." Accessed January 19, 2021. https://www.dictionary.com/e/gender-sexuality/positionality/.

Sammon, David. "Understanding Sense-Making." In *Encyclopedia of Decision Making and Decision Support Technologies,* edited by Adam Frédéric and Patrick Humphreys, 916–921. Hershey: Information Science Reference, 2008.

CHAPTER 2

Bardugo, Leigh. *Six of Crows.* New York City: Square Fish, 2018.

Peters, Jeremy W. "In a Divided Era, One Thing Seems to Unite: Political Anger." *The New York Times,* August 17, 2018. https:// www.nytimes.com/2018/08/17/us/politics/political-fights.html.

Rowling, J.K. *Harry Potter and the Prisoner of Azkaban.* New York City: Scholastic, 1999.

Shannon, Samantha. *The Priory of the Orange Tree.* London: Bloomsbury Publishing, 2019.

CHAPTER 3

Berthoz, Alain. "The Human Brain 'Projects' upon the World, Simplifying Principles and Rules for Perception." In *Neurobiology of "Umwelt": How Living Beings Perceive the World*, edited by Alain Berthoz and Yves Christen, 17–27. New York: Springer, 2010.

Brown, Tammy L. "Celebrate Women's Suffrage, but Don't Whitewash the Movement's Racism." Web log. *ACLU* (blog). American Civil Liberties Union, August 24, 2018. https://www.aclu.org/blog/womens-rights/celebrate-womens-suffrage-dont-whitewash-movements-racism.

Green, David. "Simple thinking in a complex world is a recipe for disaster." The Conversation, December 14, 2016. Accessed January 23, 2021. https://theconversation.com/simple-thinking-in-a-complex-world-is-a-recipe-for-disaster-69718.

Milligan, Susan. "Stepping Through History: A timeline of women's rights from 1769 to the 2017 Women's March on Washington." *US News & World Report,* January 20, 2017. https://www.usnews.com/news/the-report/articles/2017-01-20/timeline-the-womens-rights-movement-in-the-us

Owens, Cassie. "Our attention spans are shrinking. Here's why that matters." *The Philadelphia Inquirer,* April 25, 2019. https://www.inquirer.com/news/short-attention-span-humans-study-journalism-media-20190425.html.

Ross, Joann M. "Making marital rape visible: A history of American legal and social movements criminalizing rape in marriage." (2015).

CHAPTER 4

Brocchetto, Marilia, and Emanuella Grinberg. "Quest to Change Columbus Day to Indigenous People's Day Sails Ahead." CNN. CNN Worldwide, October 10, 2016. https://www.cnn.com/2016/10/09/us/columbus-day-indigenous-peoples-day/index.html.

de las Casas, Bartolomé. *A Short Account of the Destruction of the Indies.* London: Penguin Classics, 1999.

Davis, Kenneth C. *Don't Know Much About the American Presidents.* New York City: Hachette Books, 2012.

HowardZinn.org. "Biography." September 15, 2020. Accessed January 22,2021. https://www.howardzinn.org/about/biography/.

HowardZinn.org. "Zinn Education Project." August 29, 2020. Accessed January 22,2021. https://www.howardzinn.org/related-projects/zinn-education-project/.

Greenberg, David. "How to Make Sense of the Shocking New MLK Documents." *Politico Magazine,* June 4, 2019. https://www.politico.com/magazine/story/2019/06/04/how-to-make-sense-of-the-shocking-new-m.lk-documents-227042.

Said, Edward. *Orientalism.* New York City: Pantheon Books, 1978.

Shakespeare, William. *The Tempest.* New York City: Simon & Schuster, 2004.

Zinn, Howard, and Anthony Arnove. "Introduction to the Thirty-Fifth Anniversary Edition of a People's History of the United States." Introduction. In *A People's History of the United States*, xx. New York: Harper, 2017.

CHAPTER 5

Resnick, Brian. "The American Idea: Why Do We Hate Each Other?" *The Atlantic,* November 10, 2011. theatlantic.com/national/archive/2011/11/the-american-idea-why-do-we-hate-each-other/248205/

Sokol, Jason. "The North isn't better than the South: The real history of modern racism and segregation above the Mason-Dixon line." Salon. December 14, 2014. Accessed January 25, 2020. https://www.salon.com/2014/12/14/the_north_isnt_better_than_the_south_the_real_history_of_modern_racism_and_segregation_above_the_mason_dixon_line/.

@thenamesO. "YOU ARE NOT BETTER THAN PEOPLE IN THE SOUTH—THREAD!" Twitter. July 9, 2020. https://twitter.com/thenameso/status/1281244981257175045.

Zinn, Howard. *The Southern Mystique.* Boston: South End Press, 2002.

CHAPTER 6

Waldmeir, Patti. "I Heart the Heartlands: In Defense of the US's Misunderstood Midwest." *The Financial Times,* January 16, 2020. https://www.ft.com/content/88d2beee-372e-11ea-a6d3-9a26f8c3cba4.

CHAPTER 7

Flynn, D.J., Brendan Nyhan, and Jason Reifler. "The Nature and Origins of Misperceptions: Understanding False and Unsupported Beliefs About Politics." *Political Psychology* 38, no. 51 (January 2017): 13. https://doi.org/10.1111/pops.12394.

Foucault, Michel. *Discipline & Punish: The Birth of the Prison.* Translated by Alan Sheridan. New York City: Vintage Books, 1995.

Jilani, Zaid and Jeremy Adam Smith. "What Is the True Cost of Polarization in America?" *Greater Good Magazine,* March 4, 2019. https://greatergood.berkeley.edu/article/item/what_is_the_true_cost_of_polarization_in_america.

McLeod, Saul. "Social Identity Theory." Simply Psychology. Accessed January 26, 2021. https://www.simplypsychology.org/social-identity-theory.html.

Merriam-Webster.com Dictionary. s.v. "polarization." Accessed January 26, 2021, https://www.merriam-webster.com/dictionary/polarization.

CHAPTER 8

BBC News. "FBI: Spike in US hate crimes for third year in a row." Accessed January 27, 2021. https://www.bbc.com/news/world-us-canada-46189391.

Deaton, Jeremy. "In America, Politics Is the New Religion." Quartz, March 26, 2018. Accessed January 27, 2021. https://qz.com/1237473/in-america-politics-is-the-new-religion/.

Florida, Richard. "America's 'Big Sort' Is Only Getting Bigger." Bloomberg City Lab. Bloomberg, October 25, 2016. https://www.bloomberg.com/news/articles/2016-10-25/how-the-big-sort-is-driving-political-polarization.

Gray, Arielle. "This Boston Collective Laid the Groundwork for Intersectional Black Feminism." WBUR, June 10, 2019. Accessed January 27, 2021. https://www.wbur.org/artery/2019/06/10/boston-combahee-river-collective-intersectional-black-feminism.

Jilani, Zaid and Jeremy Adam Smith. "What Is the True Cost of Polarization in America?" *Greater Good Magazine,* March 4, 2019. https://greatergood.berkeley.edu/article/item/what_is_the_true_cost_of_polarization_in_america.

Kuper, Simon. "Loneliness Is Contributing to Our Increasingly Tribal Politics." *The Financial Times,* January 18, 2018. https://www.ft.com/content/89f16688-fb15-11e7-a492-2c9be7f3120a.

Martinovich, Milenko. "Americans' Partisan Identities Are Stronger Than Race and Ethnicity, Stanford Scholar Finds." Stanford News, August 31, 2017. Accessed January 27, 2021. https://news.stanford.edu/2017/08/31/political-party-identities-stronger-race-religion/.

Merriam-Webster.com Dictionary. s.v. "identity politics." Accessed January 27, 2021. https://www.merriam-webster.com/dictionary/polarization.

Pew Research Center—US Politics and Policy. "Partisanship and Political Animosity in 2016." Pew Research Center, August 28, 2020. https://www.pewresearch.org/politics/2016/06/22/partisanship-and-political-animosity-in-2016/.

Prokop, Andrew, and Anand Katakam. "Our Increasingly Polarized Presidency, in One Chart." Vox, February 16, 2015. Accessed January 27, 2021. https://www.vox.com/2015/2/16/8046077/presidents-polarizing-chart.

Rainie, Lee, Scott Keeter, and Andrew Perrin. "Americans' Trust in Government, Each Other, Leaders." Pew Research Center—US Politics and Policy, September 18, 2020.

Turner, Bambi. "The Ultimate Space Race Quiz." How Stuff Works. Accessed June 13, 2016. http://science.howstuffworks.com/space-race-quiz.htm.

Walker, Richard. "Political Polarization—a Dispatch from the Scholarly Front Lines." *Issues in Governance Studies*, Special Edition (December 2006): 3. https://www.brookings.edu/wp-content/uploads/2016/06/20061208.pdf.

CHAPTER 9

ACLED. "Demonstrations and Political Violence in American: New Data for Summer 2020." Accessed January 27, 2021. https://acleddata.com/2020/09/03/demonstrations-political-violence-in-america-new-data-for-summer-2020/.

Cilluffo, Anthony and Richard Fry. "Gen Z, Millennials and Gen X Outvoted Older Generations in 2018 Midterms." Pew Research

Center—US Politics and Policy. May 29, 2019. https://www.pewresearch.org/fact-tank/2019/05/29/gen-z-millennials-and-gen-x-outvoted-older-generations-in-2018-midterms/.

TEDx Talks. "Moving Beyond Cynicism: Creating the World We Want to See | Pascal Murphy | TEDxRyersonU." August 24, 2016. Video, 15:48. https://www.youtube.com/watch?v=TzoPA-5XfYp8.

Tulp, Sophia. "5 Nonprofits that Are Changing the World—All Led by Young People." YR Media, August 17, 2018. Accessed January 27, 2021. https://yr.media/news/5-nonprofits-led-by-young-people/.

CONCLUSION

ContraPoints. "The Left | ContraPoints." September 24. 2017. Video, 14:01. https://www.youtube.com/watch?v=QuN6GfUix7c.

Made in the USA
Coppell, TX
10 February 2022

73279380R10105